MW01206104

DEBT NINJAS

The Big Stick

P Michael Yates
© Debt Ninjas 2023

Debt Ninjas
info@debt-ninjas.com
debtninjas@gmail.com

Legal Disclaimer
Although the author has made every effort to ensure that the information in this book was correct at time of publishing, the author does not assume and hereby disclaims any liability for any loss, damage, or disruption caused by errors or omissions, whether such errors or omissions result from negligence, accident, or any other cause. This book is not intended as a substitute for legal advice or advice of legal professionals. The reader should consult a qualified professional on matters of legality.

For all the children.
We're trying to fix this world piece by painful piece,
so you might have a better time of it than we are

"Banking is a system that has the capacity to bring a whole country to its knees."
Niall Ferguson (Financial Historian)

"Banks have a social responsibility to contribute to the well-being of society, but often they prioritize short-term profits over long-term stability."
Christine Lagarde
(Managing Director of the International Monetary Fund)

"Banking institutions are more dangerous to our liberties than standing armies."
Andrew Jackson (Former President of the United States)

"Banks have a long history of manipulating the rules and gaming the system for their own benefit."
Sheila Bair (Former Chair of the U.S. Federal Deposit Insurance Corporation)

"The banking industry is an industry of high privilege and low integrity."
Ralph Nader (Consumer Advocate)

"Banking was conceived in iniquity and was born in sin."
Josiah Stamp (Former Director of the Bank of England)

"Banks are the leeches of society, feeding off the hard work of others."
Paul Volcker (12th chairman of the Federal Reserve)

"Banking is a legalized form of organized crime."
Ferdinand Pecora
(American lawyer and New York State Supreme Court Judge)

"Bankers are the real parasites, sucking the life out of the economy and leaving it in ruins."
Dean Baker
(Centre for Economic and Policy Research with Mark Weisbrot)

"Banking is a Ponzi scheme on a global scale, with banks as the masterminds."
Michael R. Taylor

"Bankers are economic hitmen, destroying countries and exploiting their resources."
John Perkins (Economic Hitman)

"Banking is a rigged game where the odds are always stacked against the average person."
Naomi Klein

"Bankers are modern-day highway robbers, stealing from the masses with impunity."
Michael Moore (American filmmaker, author and left-wing activist)

"Banks are the masters of illusion, creating money out of nothing and making us believe in its value."
Ellen Brown
(American author, political candidate, attorney, public speaker)

"Bankers are financial terrorists, destroying lives and economies for their own gain."
Max Keiser

"Banking is a game where the bankers always win, and the rest of us are left to suffer the consequences."
David Graeber

"Banks have become too big to fail and too powerful to control."
Joseph Stiglitz (American New Keynesian economist, public policy analyst, and professor at Columbia University)

"Banks are the gatekeepers of inequality, ensuring that wealth stays concentrated in the hands of a few."
Robert Reich
(American professor, author, lawyer, political commentator)

"Bankers are the true parasites of our economy, sucking the wealth out of the productive sectors."
Yanis Varoufakis (Greek Minister of Finance)

"Banks are vultures feeding off the carcasses of working-class families."
Elizabeth Warren (American politician and former law professor)

"Banking is a system that rewards the few at the expense of the many."
Bernie Sanders (American politician)

Contents

Introduction

This book came about as a direct result of my previous work The Title is Unimportant and its generation of many varied and diverse conversations.

In that book, the covering of the situation with the finance and credit scenario was reasonably deep, and exposed some of the many methods used by banks and credit card companies to manipulate us into a position that isn't necessarily in line with our best interests – 'interest' being the appropriate word when talking about the finance sector.

Exposing the shenanigans at play was a relatively simple task as there's no shortage of quotes, examples in the press, huge legal tomes actually telling us what should be happening, and case law showing that banks are indeed very often up to no good.

Providing a way out of our situation with them was always going to be the easy part of the equation, as the law is very clear on much of what's going on and considering I've spent the best part of twenty years studying, testing, and tweaking, it was a relative no-brainer to lay out the groundwork and work through the situation.

The method used in that book is just one of many options you can arrive at just by reading contract law. And therein lies the rub. The average man and woman hardly has a minute to sit and read, away from the entirely manufactured pressures of modern life. Ever thought that this situation might be precisely engineered this way? When we do get a minute – we don't often choose a boring book on law or wading through the hugely thrilling prospect of unraveling the enormous body of legislation on the government website. But if you're nosey (like me), and do find the impetus to commit to study, it doesn't take very long to realise that the entirety of their game – any game where people come into an agreement together; relies on a contract. That contract, is subject to rigorous rules that have been pushed and pulled at over very many years, and are now universally agreed upon, under the doctrine of fair play.

By extension, I, and probably you, eventually arrive at the next hugely boring pursuit of examining contracts that we have in order to fully grasp the rules. With modern contracts we often discover that significant parts of those rules have been ignored, as invariably, one of the parties to it (especially corporate entities) generally tries to 'get one over' on the other.

After a period of perusing said contracts, those armed with a comprehensive understanding of the rules can, with careful application of said rules, effectively unravel the alleged contract to a point where everything about it must be questioned. And once questioned with an eye on how it *should* be, we can often (always) move an errant contractor into a position where the agreement can be shown positively to be worthless due to its failure to adhere to the fair play principles.

The method in The Title is Unimportant successfully pushes back the banks, credit card companies and debt collection agencies when they attempt to shake us down for monies *they* believe are owed to them under a contract or agreement that *they* believe binds us to them and them to us.

(There's a *lot* of belief involved with credit creation and fortunately, that's mostly all it is, as not much of it can be proven satisfactorily enough to warrant any kind of enforcement).

All of the information used in my work is in the public domain, available via legislation (if you can plough through the jargon and 'non-English' that's often used) and pretty much all books on contract law expound on the many tools we have available with which to flush out a less than legitimate agreement.

And of course, for those inclined to run with the information, it isn't too much of a stretch to see how this method can be adapted and applied to virtually any kind of money-grab situation that presents itself to us.

The power of contract law and it's far reaching, self-evident principles, will quickly seep into your daily life as if you already owned it (which actually, you do). You'll arrive at a mindset that presents a set of common sense, logical, governing thought processes as a default mindset with regard to dealing with bogus claimants on your hard-earned commercial tokens.

Many detailed books have been written stretching back hundreds of years covering the sometimes complex aspects of the contracting process, and while there are a number of important aspects to it, each with their own pros and cons, it just wasn't necessary to cover all of it in 'The Title', as really, it only takes a very basic understanding of the rudiments to dismantle most modern contracts and that's because most, if not all, are flawed in some way. Imperfect process seems to be the way it's done these days – which is somewhat fortunate for those wishing to get out of them and not so much for those wanting to enforce them.

The success of what we're doing isn't evidenced by anything as obvious as a full public confession by the bank or DCA (Debt Collection Agency) in their writing to us and conceding; no, it is evidenced by a) their failure to move the case into a courtroom to gain enforcement, b) defaulting to using a fake court that produces fake judgments and c) abandoning their attempts at contacting us to demand payment.

That situation, as innocuous as it sounds, is actually a significant victory, because the money we worked hard for gets to stay in our pocket, and the threatening letters cease dropping through our mailbox. So the victory is a quiet one, but it is powerful.

Up until very recently, that was the aim of the Debt Ninjas remit and it works like a charm. It *was* the best we could hope for, and that quiet victory is *almost* guaranteed as long as there's legislation and law operating at any level sufficient to keep us entertained in the notion that we have some form of restrictive control mechanism regarding the operations of banking institutions. It gets us out of the predicament basically.

Where it sometimes fails, is when a DCA engages an errant soliciting company that will bend the rules regarding what's allowed.

In Britain and other parts of the world there's a system of commercial 'courts' that basically make rubber-stamping 'judgments' for anyone that pays their fee.

There's no 'hearing' as such and on several occasions I requested to be present in the courtroom when the case was heard – only to be told that they had no facility for that to happen. The best they could do was a live video link while I watched as they mindlessly go about their processing. Sometimes I was asked for my defence, but it was clear from the outset that the outcome had already been determined prior to the hearing.

The Northampton County Court Business Centre (clue in the name) is not a courtroom as we would expect, but is simply a bulk clearing house where they process a staggering amount of claims in a day. They recently rebranded and are now known as the Civil National Business Centre. Note there is no mention of the word 'court' in there and I suspect that this is because they have been given the hard word by the genuine Northampton County Court that impersonating a court is treasonous and highly illegal. They'll probably rebrand again in the next four years.

In fairness, if all you do is rubber-stamp claims and produce 'county court judgments', then your ability to process thousands of claims per day is only limited to the number of staff you can employ, I guess.

The tell in this situation is apparent when it comes to the enforcement of said 'judgment'. The Civil National Business Centre have no access to Bailiffs with which to enforce the judgment simply because they are not a bona fide court and because due process has not been followed. It seems to me that if you're fair game to be rolled by these people then you're very likely to believe they have some kind of authority to take your money / possessions etc. In the end, the most they can do after 'judgment' has been passed is to put the account back onto the conveyor belt of debt collectors and endless empty claims – something we've already dealt with prior to this situation. It could be an endless cycle if we allowed it.

So at present (and for the last 300 years at the very least), contract law governs all people and their actions, especially those that would wave around imaginary contracts in their attempts to shake us down for money. Getting the foundations right at the beginning of the contract is relatively easy to accomplish with just a small amount of understanding, except for those, it would seem, that would rather maintain secretive

16

operations to produce their gain - at our loss.

As a consequence of the efforts many people are now making, which is basically just asking the right (simple) questions of the 'lenders', we're witnessing game changes on an almost daily basis, as banks and debt collectors are being forced to rewrite their communications to us to a) stay within the law (no threats please, we have protection) as they seek to make *something* stick to get us to pay; and b) attempt to coerce us into thinking that what they do is legitimate and that we have some form of liability to them.

If everything they did *was* legit, then we'd be in court before our feet touched the ground and an easy case would be won every time, simply by the claimant waving a bona fide contract under the judge's nose. But there seems to be a problem here - we aren't being invited to court by the bank, and that's a very telling situation.

This new vista is all coming into view primarily because thousands of people are now challenging the bank - who in turn are hopelessly trying to maintain their futile position; which is that they believe there is a legally binding contract between us. The facts speak loud and clear on this matter.

The alleged debt situation is relatively easy to get out of once we understand the game and begin the process. Our peace resumes in direct proportion to our growth in knowledge and confidence as we enter a new place of understanding where the psychological warfare ceases to work as it once did.

This is all fantastic news for those of us that were feeling pressured and / or hopelessly despondent about our life and the prospect of potentially enduring financial misery and hardship for the rest of it.

I always had a persistent niggle in the back of my mind regarding this situation and it was this; after the dust had settled, I was anxious for a way to restore the karmic side of the equation (because there is a karmic side to all of this). My biggest question was always 'how can these organisations do what they do and get away with selling the account, closing the file, and then continuing their business as usual?' Whilst simultaneously totally screwing up our right to create credit, access commercial tokens and render us powerless. Why aren't they reigned in and punished for their actions?

When we 'politely' requested that they substantiate their claims against us, the bank went into full Berserker mode and lashed out in all directions like an injured animal in their attempts to stop us from doing exactly what we're required to do under law. They inflicted significant damage to our credit file - literally crippling our commercial standing and producing a situation that hangs around our neck like a millstone and interferes with our right to engage in commercial activity for a long time.

I'm sure the banks think they're covered when they state "it's an automatic process" and "we can't do anything to stop it", but I disagree rigorously as it all happens DURING the time that we're attempting to correct the situation and remain in honour.

So ideally, (if it were a fair situation) there should be in-built mechanisms that activate automatically and halt the process until the situation is resolved – again, this is actually a requirement under contracting law.

In the end, it's no big deal really, as it serves as a dead giveaway that they're already on the back-foot and this behaviour, combined with their deception and fraud at the outset, is what's always annoyed me deeply. Essentially it's nothing more than playground bully mentality.

At some point the credit file miraculously gets corrected without any notification, and if we don't keep checking it - we'll never know. And waiting around for some form of apology or 'Restitution' is like waiting for a compulsive liar to 'fess up - actually it isn't like that – that's exactly what it is!

Many people, having read the first book and engaging with the process invariably arrived at that question and the Debt Ninja mailbox began to pile up. This lead to new research with a deeper focus. The new questions became "How can this situation be resolved and corrected quickly? How do we apply retribution? How do we make the bank acknowledge their unacceptable conduct and make reparations for the situation they put us in?" "How do I fix my credit file?"

It quickly became apparent that getting the bank's confession to what they'd done was my goal, because frankly, if you or I acted like that in business there'd be all manner of lawsuits flying at us from every direction.

This 'one rule for them, and one for us' situation is untenable and must stop if we are to consider ourselves a caring and intelligent species. That one set of humans can make life unbearable for another is about as low, and genuinely barbaric as it's possible to reach.

The banks are without doubt a cartel. They operate in secrecy, regularly flout the law (as can be seen almost daily), and conspire together to extract unimaginable amounts of energy from us all, that they then convert into spendable tokens of the day – the currency. And in the meantime they direct the policy of actual countries and their people via political influence and buying power. I know that this situation is well understood and acknowledged by most people so I'll not dwell on it as we all know that it must change.

As stated in 'The Title is Unimportant', a remedy was being worked on that would hopefully bear fruit in the not too distant future, and it would seem, that that day has arrived. A remedy has been found (they always are) and it is so strong it needs its own volume to convey the scope and intricacies.

Whilst quite a lengthy process, it remains very simple (as they always are) and enormously interesting, as finally, those that have been mistreated by the banking establishment (basically all of us) will soon possess the tools needed to access restitution to our standing and a fair, just, and reasonable return to our proper status.

This book is being written whilst simultaneously testing the method, so will obviously evolve as new study reveals more tools and the results come in. Having said that I am 100% convinced that this remedy WILL bear the fruit we seek, because basically, under the law it must.

There isn't a single part of this work that relies on conjecture, prayer, or a weak hope that some benefactor-type hero of the people will swoop in and correct the entire weight of injustice in the world, put naughty people in jail and give everyone lots of money – all while draining the swamp and publishing 'the list'.

Everything here comes directly from the legislation, common and case law, and the huge tomes of legal treatise over the years that have been written by the heavy hitters such as Judges, Lord Chief Justice's and law professors in their endeavours to clarify and carve out the rules (that have subsequently been hugely perverted in recent times).

Those rules are still there and available to all who seek them, though the obfuscation of most of it has been the work of ages for those that would rather we didn't know.

The resolution was always going to be a matter of taking it back to law and applying the legislation provided, and that's where most people have failed.

Reading legislation is immensely boring – unless you're looking for something specific (which we are) and the great majority of banks have placed a significant amount of reliance on our not reading it, to the point where they're now openly in breach of most of it with aplomb. "It'll be okay, they're too lazy and stupid to figure it all out - so we're safe". Well, we'll see about that very soon.

As it turned out none of the legislation and law texts are prohibitively complicated at all, and is for the most part just basic common sense.

The component parts of this remedy fuse together to produce a clear and damning case against the banks / credit card company, debt collector etc. and on the face of it, will give our adversaries a difficult time in trying to dodge our claims once we have them perfected and aimed accurately.

And let's not forget that in all of this there's always the very real potential for the defendant to buy a Judge to skew the case and give a verdict they require. It happens – I've seen it on several occasions! Happily though, even that scenario has a remedy within the law.

The book idea came out of a succession of discussions with John Kelso as we batted back-and-forth with all the various ways that remedy could be articulated to combat the many and varied scenarios that people are facing on a daily basis under what we all know is a heavily-biased system. We postulated scenario after scenario and played Devil's advocate to each other's ideas, presenting situations that might arise where the bank might scrape together a proper defence to our claims.

Again, the good news is that case law illustrates much of what we imagined might be presented by way of a defence, and promptly demolishes it - which came as a significant resolve-stiffener. If we follow 'due process' throughout (which is their rules) then they will be exposed and defenseless as no matter how good their lawyers are, they cannot easily go against legal processes and due process.

The research is ongoing and extensive and produces nuggets everyday. Within the first two days of scouring Acts of Parliament we found to our surprise that much of it covers what we needed and some of it fitted our needs exactly. The bonus was learning that it *can* be aimed with absolute precision at our tormentors.

It was also discovered that using case law in a court scenario (should that scenario arise), we can completely remove a Judge's discretion. Judges love case law because it gives them an easy time of the situation without them having to think for themselves. They just follow what happened before and make the same determination as the case law.

If there's ever an instance where a Judge wants to make a name for themselves by going against precedent, and creating new case law, this work will present a horrific scenario for them as they attempt to a challenge to a 'Lord Justice's deliverance'.

The approach to this method is expectedly multi-faceted (when is there a situation where it isn't?) but everything converges into a point of precision to produce a literal 'big stick' to hit the bank (or DCA) with.

A significant part of this strategy is to establish and

prove for the record that the bank engaged in less-than-legal behaviour from the outset and proceeded on an unlawful / illegal footing from there.

Many things have happened since we 'agreed' to do business with them and, via legislation, law and heavyweight legal tomes used in the courts, we can now launch our charges at them.

The bank's activities include, but as we are finding daily, are not limited to:

1. Deception

2. Failure to disclose

3. Misappropriation

4. Misrepresentation

5. Concealment

6. Commercial damage

7. Defamation

8. Embezzlement

9. Data protection breach

10. Larceny / Theft

11. Unjust enrichment

12. Money Laundering

13. Cybercrime

14. Racketeering

15. Insurance Fraud

16. Harassment

It's quite the list and some charges are immediately apparent while others are less obvious, but all are applicable at some level.

To address the charges we can cite many breaches of legislation on their part and these include:

1. The Fraud Act 2006

2. The Criminal Finances Act 2017

3. The Torts Act 1977

4. The Bank of England and Financial Services Act 2016

5. The Modern Slavery Act 2015

6. The Defamation Act 2013

7. The Financial Services Act 2012

8. The Misrepresentation Act 1967

9. The Malicious Communications Act 1988

10. The Data Protection Act 2018

11. The Companies Act 2006

12. The Protection from Harassment Act 1997

13. The Theft Act 1968

In addition to those, there are several Common Law breaches, the most notable being Unjust Enrichment.

Using legislation as our baseline this book aims cite the pertinent points of each aspect and detail the ways in which the bank and credit card company have routinely defied these rules to produce a situation that is *always* to the detriment of the men & women that believe they are entering into a bona fide agreement with these supposed bastions of decency and trustworthiness.

It can now be clearly demonstrated that these financial institutions aren't anywhere near the respectability they hope to convey, and so it should reasonably be expected that this work will trigger firstly anger at what has been done, followed quickly by the desire to claim our restoration and seek remedy for what has been done to all of us for very many years.

The by-product of all this process will undoubtedly lead to further distrust and likely significant damage to the banking system as we know it, and may even force a correction on a scale unlike we've ever seen. It might even usher-in the long-overdue overhaul that the banking system should've had many years ago.

In the end, the banks will benefit from this process – just not quite as much as they have been doing so far.

So here it is. This work is evolving daily and at the time of writing is largely theoretical but it has the added bonus of being fully backed by current legislation, common law, and plenty of case law. If all of that fails, then the systems of legislation fail and must be immediately withdrawn, as it would become self-evident at that point that legislation is worthless. *Hint – the law cannot be allowed to be seen failing.

This book is deliberately to the point, because it needs to be. There's no real need to reprint all of the legislation because that's available freely on government websites etc, and who has the time to work through a huge tome on legal remedy – assuming that we could outlay the £1400 or so that these things cost (oh, if you must, get it on a card!) This work is the digested nuggets of all of that reading to boil it down and extract the process to get to the meat of the issue, and that's the blueprint by which we're going to get the job done.
Due to the high demand for this book to be published sooner rather than later, there *will* be errors and omissions but as with all works of this nature, corrections will occur and updates will be frequent.

There is also *repetition* throughout, as the restating of

principles and methods helps reinforcement and cementing previously complex material into the mind.

Watch this space.

Chapter One

What has the bank actually been doing?

Aside from creating and deploying the never-ending psychological manipulation that began in our early childhood via our parents' reinforcement, the banking system has compiled quite the list of naughty maneuvers it uses when dealing with its customers – read 'victims'.

Thankfully there aren't too many people these days that maintain a blissful ignorance of bank shenanigans, and most are entirely unsurprised to hear of yet another banking scandal breaking in the daily news. It really seems to be an endless catalogue of underhand activity and never ceases to amaze that most people still assume that whatever the latest story of how this or that bank has manipulated a situation in its favour, they'll remain unaffected, and the bank deserve everything that's coming to them now they've been caught.

Well yes, the banks deserve everything they get (and likely a lot more) when caught, but there's a much bigger scenario brewing in the background and a tidal wave is coming towards them, and isn't showing any signs of stopping.

A feeling that will likely appear during the reading of this book is that this is all very personal and somewhat hurtful, and that's mainly because it IS personal. As the facts are laid out revealing the nature of the behaviour ALL banks and most financial institutions are engaged in, on their never-ending quest to relieve us of our energy -that'd be YOU, ME, and everyone else that has ever done any business with a bank or credit card company, so yes, it's personal.

The course of action we take once at the point of becoming fully aware of the things we didn't know beforehand, is entirely up to us, but chances are that you, like me, will want to re-balance the scales as quickly as possible and give them something back by way of a metaphorical kick in the balls for what they've done. After all, the lavish lifestyle of executive bankers is not gained through honest endeavours and a fair day's work; it is gained through direct exploitation of customers in a parasitic extraction / conversion process that they keep very quiet about.

That extraction procedure would be acceptable (to a point), IF the resulting benefits were shared with the creators of the capital i.e. us; but they are not, and the great majority of banking victims are demonstrably

NOT living the same kind of lifestyle that the bank's executive level enjoy.

Sure, we could all enter the banking profession and work our way up the executive level (as if…) but even if we did do that, and everything turned out very nice thank you - it still doesn't excuse the practice.

So regarding our search for the method of correction, we found that the rules are laid out very clearly in the legislation of practically every country in the world and provide fertile grounds for applying our remedy.

Legislation exists for the protection of all that require it, conditional on either finding a legal person that is onside with our cause, or following a thorough understanding and knowledge of its deployment.

Let's face it - we do ALL want it, but the problem as always, is that most people are lazy and can't be bothered to read complex material and much less execute it. It *is* quite a hefty read after all and even if people weren't lazy and / or complacent, legislation is a hard thing to read for the average man and woman, and even harder to understand without a bit of legal knowledge. Is that perhaps deliberate I wonder?

Whatever the case may be, reading through an Act, statute or code is a daunting prospect, because it's very boring to say the least, and understanding it is predictably difficult.

And then we have the law books, as used in courtrooms the world over by judges and legal personnel. These are huge doorsteps of legal…stuff. Case law and 'treatise' compiled by judges and lawyers, professors, barristers and high-level experts in the field over several hundreds of years.

This material is actually easier to read than legislation, but getting hold of the exact books used by the profession is eye-wateringly expensive (and thanks must go again to those altruistic benefactors such as Barclaycard, Capital One, Amex etc.)

So the learning curve began and very quickly it was realised, mostly unsurprisingly, that the banks are even worse than we first thought.

What they've been doing became self-evident, as did what we can use to claim our restitution.

Simultaneously, that smug / peaceful / empowered feeling arrived when it was understood that we *can* take them to task on pretty much every aspect of their behaviour towards us.

Once the bank is presented with an extensive catalogue of accusations it should become glaringly obvious (and quickly) that it wouldn't behoove them to attempt a denial of what they've done (but they will…right to the end!). Their system has been operating in this way for a very long time - probably as long as much of the contract law they routinely breach, and so claiming not to have any knowledge of what they're doing would be committing a huge disservice to their clearly brilliant progenitors of the scam back in the day. And let's not forget the good 'ole phrase "ignorance of the law is no excuse".

The game is almost up, and all that remains to be seen is how they will deal with being caught.

So let's call a thing a thing shall we, and have a cursory look at their activities before really getting into the nitty gritty of it.

Deception

From the very outset of our relationship with the bank they operated in a way that a parasite might view a potential host. Their reason d'être is to extract our energy in a way that's 'we're big and mighty and you should feel honoured that we might deign to speak to you and possibly offer our help". And whilst none of that sentiment is overtly expressed, it's always there in the background. From the point of our first contact, the psychology machine gears up and leads us to a merry tune down the garden path of belief system reinforcement.

Much of the deception employed by the bank towards us is in the form of their failure to disclose information that's crucial to the contracting process. It could be a simple oversight - an accidental situation, or maybe not, because really, after such a long time in the game they've clearly had plenty of opportunity to get their operations straight enough to fall within the law.

After picking apart all of the process involved when we go 'cap-in-hand' to get some credit, I know fully that none of it is accidental - after all, despots and control-freaks hardly shy away from opportunities to increase their status and level of control. With the bank it's always the same routine, so there's a definite element of 'business-as-usual' going on here, and disclosure never happens - it's as simple as that.

When we fill out the paperwork at the start of the process, the bank, 100% of the time, fails to disclose that we're creating a security instrument or, a specie of CASH. That this is the case, is no secret to those in the know, in fact there's plenty of case law and banker statements confirming that this is indeed true, but unfortunately most people just don't look into it that deeply to find out – why would they?

The bank then fails to disclose – or makes it very hard to comprehend, that the completion of the paperwork conveys rights to the bank to use our property (the security instrument) without permission and without our knowledge. It's all very covertly worded in the smallest of small print.

The bank fail to disclose that our completed agreement is accepted by them as a promissory note – a cheque.

The value of the securitised note is then added to their ledger as a profit and they fail to disclose that.

They fail to disclose that they bundle our security with many others and sell them on the securities markets to investors - for profit.

They fail to disclose anywhere to buyers that those

securities are NOT theirs to trade – as in, original issue.

They fail to disclose that they take out an insurance policy on the account in case we fail to pay.

Based on that insurance policy, they then fail to disclose that they're now engaged in a conflict of interests. They win if we pay *and* if we don't.

They fail to disburse profits gained from trading our property (the security).

They fail to disburse interest gained on profits made from our property.

They fail to disclose that no money is moved from their side to ours, and that our security instrument is used to create the credit.

They knowingly expanded our belief that something was lent to us by them.

There's also the issue of tax on the profits gained from trading securities. Do they pay tax on their gains as is required? (This is being looked into currently).

So there's quite the trail of deception here for our first meeting with them.

Fraud in contract

Fraud in contract is the intentional misrepresentation or concealment of material facts by one or more parties in a contractual agreement, with the aim of inducing another party to enter into the contract; that then leads to financial harm or losses by one (or more) party.

The overarching definition of fraud is "a deceptive and illegal act carried out by an individual or organisation to gain financial or personal benefits through deceit, trickery, or manipulation."

Essentially, fraud undermines the fundamental principles of contractual agreements; it erodes trust and ultimately distorts the fairness of the deal.

There are two common types of fraud in contract and they are misrepresentation and non-disclosure.

Fraud is serious, and can result in significant financial and legal consequences for the party engaged in such conduct, and when we examine our alleged contract with the bank in more depth, holding it up to the light of contracting rules as it were, we see almost immediately that it's not just full of holes - it's actually made of mesh. The entire situation is nothing *but* fraud.

Most, if not all of the components required for a legitimate and legally binding *enforceable* contract agreement between parties, are not present and I suspect the banks are fully aware of this and will continue this way as long as there are takers for their offer.

Misrepresentation

In law, misrepresentation is a statement made by one or more of the parties involved that is untrue or misleading, and is made with the intention of inducing the other parties to enter into the contract. It can be made either by words, actions, or by silence.

The misrepresentation must also be material, meaning that it must be an important factor in inducing the other party to enter into the contract.

There are different types of fraudulent misrepresentation in contract law:

1. Innocent misrepresentation
   This is when a party makes a statement that is untrue, but they genuinely believe it to be true.

2. Negligent misrepresentation
   This is when a party makes a statement without taking reasonable care to ensure its accuracy.

3. Fraudulent misrepresentation
   This occurs when a party makes a statement that they know is untrue or misleading, and with the intention of inducing the other party to enter into the contract.

Number one; innocent misrepresentation applies to lower level banking staff as they genuinely believe that the bank lends their own or customer's deposited money to make loans to a credit account. The problem here is that staff are well trained by the bank and the training either intentionally or accidentally failed to inform them of what's really going on. Most, if not all customer-facing staff members are genuinely of the belief that the bank lends money and that's how the wheels keep turning - because they don't read banking law.

Innocent misrepresentation also provides staff with plausible deniability for their actions. They're still liable to some degree however, as one should know precisely what they are involved in especially in matters that impact the lives of others. Innocent misrepresentation doesn't exonerate the bank's CEO and executive staff though, as they are implicitly involved and have a mandate of 'the duty of care' for the actions of every employee of the organisation as well as its customers.

Number two; negligent misrepresentation applies to all banking staff because every member of any organisation should be fully aware of what they're involved in. Perhaps in the near future there'll be an explosion of claims against the bank's CEO from its lower level staff members for involving them in the deceit and thereby putting their reputation and livelihoods at risk. Every staff member at the bank is trained to do their job, and during that training it wouldn't take too much effort on the bank's behalf to correct childhood indoctrination and set the record straight.

As it stands, that belief system is rigorously reinforced by the training schedule. It isn't until they approach the executive levels that the truth might be revealed and I would guess that the selection process for those positions is largely based upon the candidate's propensity for being bound to secrecy.

Number three; fraudulent misrepresentation applies to the executive level directly. They know fully what they're involved in, and if they don't, then an immediate inquiry directed at their boss is in order. The CEO of the bank is in full knowledge of the 'unspoken' rules of the game. They wouldn't be a very good CEO if there were crucial aspects of the company's operation that were unknown to them. The CEO is entirely responsible for every action their employees make (as with any other company) through their liability bond. Everyone working in every business operates under the umbrella policy of the CEO as a matter of trading law.

Directors immediately below the CEO must also know what's going on and there are no excuses, because someone at that level wouldn't take very long at all to realise that something is amiss, just by the one fact that the bank makes a disproportionate amount of profit from very little outlay. Where do they think their outrageous bonuses come from? That they do nothing once in possession of this knowledge makes them complicit – especially for taking payouts while in full knowledge of what the gig is.

The bank engages in misrepresentation from the outset. We create and give them a valuable security instrument and they bring nothing to the table that was theirs. The entire deal is heavily biased against us.

The bank then proceeds to extract monies from us in full knowledge that they have no legal basis to do so, because the contract is void under law, but they continue regardless.

If we figure out the scam and stop making the monthly payments to the account, as is required of everyone under contract rules, the bank (and every subsequent third-party after them) proceeds to inflict damage to our commercial standing via our credit file.

They fail to sign the agreement as a man or woman and instead, either don't sign it or sign as the bank's name. This is illegal as only living men & women can contract with each other.

So it would seem reasonably logical at this point to assume that the bank pins a sizeable amount of hope on our being sufficiently uneducated on the very laws enacted to protect us from such behaviour by these alleged good faith and honourable institutions. Or perhaps they're just more pompous than we already thought, and truly believe they're untouchable?

Non-Disclosure

This comprises the intentional withholding of crucial information that could affect the decision-making process of the other party. This form of fraud commonly arises in situations where one party possesses superior knowledge or expertise, and also when individuals deliberately conceal material information that, if revealed, would significantly impact the decision-making process of another party. While fraud by non-disclosure may seem less obvious than other forms of fraud, its ethical implications and legal consequences can be profound.

It usually occurs in situations where individuals have a duty to disclose material facts as being relevant to the full understanding of the deal.

Fraud by non-disclosure raises significant ethical concerns as intrinsic principles such as honesty, transparency, and fairness are violated when material information is withheld. By depriving others of the opportunity to make informed decisions, those perpetrating fraud by non-disclosure demonstrate an absolute lack of respect for autonomy and a total disregard for the potential consequences of their actions.

The ethical responsibility to disclose crucial information arises from the fundamental principle of non-maleficence. It requires these individuals to prevent harm or minimise potential risks, and by withholding information, they engage in fraud by non-disclosure and knowingly expose others to financial, emotional, or physical harm, and violate their obligation.

Legal recourse for fraud by non-disclosure may also include criminal charges depending on the jurisdiction and the severity of the case. Punishments can range from fines and restitution, to imprisonment, particularly in cases where the fraudulent act causes significant harm or is part of a larger criminal scheme.

Concealment

Fraud by concealment, also known as fraudulent concealment, is where an individual intentionally hides or withholds important information from another party in order to deceive them.

In this setting, the individual committing the fraud may make false statements or representations, but the key element is *deliberately* withholding information that the other party has a right to know. This can involve deliberate omission to disclose important facts, or employ active efforts to hide or obscure the truth.

A typical example of fraud by concealment is when a company fails to disclose material financial information to potential investors. In such cases, the failure to disclose can result in significant financial harm to the other party.

To prove fraud by concealment, it must be shown that the individual who committed the fraud had a duty to disclose the information in question, and that they intentionally withheld or concealed that information.

Also, it must be shown that the other party suffered harm as a result of the concealment. In our case with the bank, it's fairly obvious that they deliberately withheld critical information during the agreement stage. Had we known about their true intentions and the subsequent gains they were about to make by doing business with us (read doing business 'to' us) then we might've rethought the whole situation or at least made efforts to reframe the deal to be less biased in the bank's favour.

Fraud by concealment is a serious offence and usually results in significant legal and financial consequences for the individual(s).

Defamation

Defamation is defined as any false statement that harms a person's reputation or character. It can take various forms, including libel (written defamation) and slander (spoken defamation). Defamation can have serious consequences, including damage to our personal and professional relationships, loss of employment, and emotional distress.

To prove defamation, the party making the claim must show that the statement in question is false, that it was communicated to a third party, and that it caused harm.

When we engage with the bank in our attempts to get answers, they begin the process of applying judgments to our commercial standing via the credit file. Or rather, they fail to halt their automatic process that sends out default judgments and reports to the credit file agency.

That they fail to halt their actions is extremely bad form as we're in the process of trying to liaise with the bank to correct the situation. Due to the bank's failures at the agreement stage to create a legitimate contract, those reports are 100% defamation.

The bank shows strong disinterest in forthright communications with us during our endeavours to resolve the matter, and their reporting to credit file agencies is literally the trashing of our good standing based on an automatic mechanism that they believe gives them a level of protection under the 'plausible deniability' framework.

Plausible Deniability usually involves the intentional creation of a situation where the person in authority can claim they were not aware of any misconduct or illegal activity, even if they *were* actually aware of it. It's usually accomplished by delegating responsibilities to others and avoiding direct involvement in questionable activities.

In the bank's case, that would be their issuing of default judgments. The person in authority can then claim that they did not have any direct knowledge or involvement in the wrongdoing, precisely because it was automatically carried out. That doesn't fly however, as they have a duty to their customers, a professional code of conduct, and not least in this, legislation to refer to, that guides against creating these sorts of incidents.

At the point of receiving our first letter (from The Title is Unimportant) the bank should engage a full investigation into the situation to establish what has occurred and only *after* a resolution has been found and agreed by the parties, can the contract resume or be terminated with all parties being notified.

Those adverse credit file entries are a deliberate sabotage to our reputation that the bank *chooses* to employ, instead of taking appropriate action, which would be to act honourably, stand accountable, and actually investigate our concerns with full reporting and subsequent correction.

Negligence

The bank fails to answer our forthright questions (often with the statement that they *will not* and are *not obliged to answer them*), and this unfortunately amounts to *secrecy*. Secrecy is not permitted under FCA (Financial Conduct Authority) rules. Their actions produce negligence towards the customer and this happens despite a strong requirement to operate in transparency under banking legislation.

Another significant aspect of the bank's negligent operations is their abject failure to sign off their communications in compliance with the Companies Act 2006 (more later).

In order for negligence to be established in a contractual context, the following elements must be present:

1. Duty of care:
   The party in question must owe and demonstrate

a duty of care to the other party under the terms of the contract. This duty of care is typically implied in all contracts, and requires that each party perform their obligations with reasonable care and skill.

2. Breach of duty:
The party in question must have breached their duty of care by failing to perform their obligations in a competent and diligent manner. This breach could be a failure to perform the obligation altogether, or it could be a substandard performance of the obligation.

3. Causation:
The breach of duty must have caused the other party to suffer some form of loss or damage. In other words, the breach must be the cause of the other party's loss.

4. Damages:
The other party must have suffered some form of loss or damage as a result of the breach of duty. This could include financial loss, damage to property, or other forms of harm... like a severely damaged credit rating?

If these elements are present, the party who breached their duty of care could be liable for damages or other forms of legal remedy. It's important to note that the standard of care required in a contractual context will vary depending on the specific circumstances of the contract and the nature of the obligations in question.

This is likely to be entirely moot however, as the contract is already voided by their actions at the very beginning of the relationship. If anything, the charge of negligence could be posited as the primary reason for their failure to validate the entire agreement.

Malicious Communications

Malicious communications applies to any form of communication that is designed to harm or cause distress to the recipient. This can include harassment, threats, cyber bullying, cyber stalking, or any other form of communication that is intended to cause a negative situation.

Default Notices, attempts to extract cash via mail, threats of court action or collection activity etc, are all forms of malicious communication. To clarify; any time there's a communication conveying a version of "…if you don't do this, then that will happen", it is a threat, and is designed purposely to motivate an action from us through fear. This is a malicious communication.

When we make our earnest attempts to engage in dialogue with the bank or DCA (Debt Collection Agency) via our letters, and they subsequently ignore everything we're saying and instead continue to make demands, they're actually in direct conflict with the legal requirements of being transparent, professional, and helpful to their customers through duty of care.

Personally, I welcome these types of communication.

Typically I wait until three letters have arrived - which eliminates any potential for their claiming a mistake has been made; because once something has happened three times, it's nearly impossible to say it was accidental. Three letters proves intent. I save these letters as it comprises *prima facie* evidence of their breaches of legislation.

Also, the fact that they are writing to us in the first instance is a direct breach of the data protection act because at this stage we can clearly demonstrate that there is no contract between the parties that they can rely upon to claim a business relationship. They have no legal authority to even hold our name and address on file, let alone write to us and make demands, so the charge of malicious communications is a low-hanging fruit in our situation.

Unjust Enrichment

Unjust enrichment is a legal concept that originated in common law. It took a while to gain traction in the legal world but has been gaining ground quickly in recent years.

Unjust Enrichment principles arise when one party unfairly benefits from another party's actions or property. It happens when one person is enriched at the expense of another in a manner that's unjust or unfair. This can happen in a variety of situations, such as when someone receives money or property that rightfully belongs to another person, or when a party is unjustly enriched by the labour or services of another party.

The legal principle is based on the idea that no one should be allowed to profit unfairly at the expense of another. When one person benefits unfairly from another's actions or property, the law requires the unjustly enriched party to return the benefit or compensate the other party appropriately.

The legal remedies available in this setting vary across jurisdictions, and common approaches include restitution, disgorgement of profits, and the imposition of a constructive trust.

Restitution, the name for the process of correcting unjust enrichment, seeks to restore the aggrieved party to their original position before the unjust enrichment occurred, ensuring that they are not left worse off due to the unfair gain of another.

Disgorgement of profits aims to strip the unjustly enriched party of any profits gained from their wrongful conduct.

Constructive trusts impose a legal obligation on the unjustly enriched party to hold the property or benefit in question for the benefit of the aggrieved party.

The bank stole our property and traded it for profit on the markets. They also took cash payments on the account (the monthly repayment amounts) and charged us interest on the 'loan' or credit, all with no legal basis to do so. This again, is a relatively simple construct to prove as evidence abounds as to our service of the alleged debt in addition to the bank's consistent failure to produce the original agreement for our inspection.

In the case of restitution it would be impossible for the bank to retrieve our long-gone security and return it to us unmarked, so the next best thing would be a payment to cover the lost / stolen / traded instrument at its assumed current value.

Enticement to Slavery

This seems a strange thing to cite when talking about modern westernised life, but in our scenario it isn't that much of a stretch to see that we are compelled to work to repay an alleged debt. That we have to do this or face the prospect of being unable to meet the 'repayments' and thus deal with the consequences; is a form of slavery. We are bound into servitude, albeit voluntarily (but done via deception), through 'agreeing' to service an arrangement that we believed at the time was a legitimate contract. We suffer through lack of understanding and are thus tied into the deal through a process of honour. We may be compelled to work for years, or even our entire lives to pay off the imaginary debt.

In our particular case, the bank stated that we must pay them until the alleged loan plus interest is cleared. That they continue to ignore our concerns and refuse to discuss the matter once we withhold payments until a resolution is found, is a breach of their duty to investigate our claims as stipulated under contract law.

Any party in a contract is *obliged* to immediately stop all process if an issue or fault is discovered in the contract, and the parties must then work either together or independently to resolve the problem.

The bank is deaf to our alerts to the problem, and continues with their demands regardless. And why wouldn't they? The gravy train has been running perfectly well this way for years.

The bank's unwillingness to engage and deal with the issue professionally, including treating us fairly and respectfully (because we actually have a genuine problem with the contract), and instead, forging ahead with their process, is direct evidence of enticement to slavery. "Nothing you do or say makes any difference to the outcome because we are right and you are wrong. We are big and you are small" is the general Matilda theme, which is exactly the same as "we aren't interested in anything you have to say, so keep working and paying us until you either die or have paid your debt". This is well defined and falls under slavery.

Commercial Damage

During the process of our attempting to negotiate with the bank, they inflict actual damage to our commercial standing. They do that by reporting defaults and negative judgments with the credit file agencies.

The bank literally destroys our credit rating for a period of up to six years, which makes commercial activity extremely difficult, or impossible. The reports by the bank, when measured against our willingness to co-operate and enter discussion (as can be evidenced by our letters), are hugely disproportionate and nothing short of malicious and spiteful. The bank becomes distanced, refuses to enter into any discussion, and instead lash out at us for daring to question anything regarding their actions. Or perhaps they just want to hit us hard enough to make us think twice about challenging them again. It's very likely a bit of both.

Criminal damage typically refers to physical damage to property but in this instance, the bank inflicts actual damage to our reputation and commercial standing producing the same effect as if we were bodily injured or physically incapacitated. We suffer an injured status. Our *person* is damaged, and we're unable to function as we once did in the commercial arena. It's exactly the same as if we endured physical damage and could no longer work. Our commercial vehicle has been crippled and all we did was discover a problem and attempt to resolve it. Patently this is *not* something the bank likes to deal with at any level.

Harm and Loss

Given the understanding of the fact that our 'person' is our commercial vehicle, for us to use in commercial activity, and that all action we undertake in the commercial world is done *through* our person, we can see how the credit file system has become a valuable tool for business, because it conveys our commercial 'worthiness'.

Our credit report informs others about our ability and willingness to conduct and maintain trustworthy business when dealing with other 'persons'. It reflects the state of our 'dependability' in much the same way that its successor the 'social credit report' will convey those details and so much more about us in the future.

In modern times the credit file has replaced our word - our honour. No longer is it deemed acceptable for someone to say "I give you my word", and that's because the business world, with it's penchant for executing unfair deals and stripping people of assets on a daily basis, has destroyed any relevance to 'my word is my bond'. In that world, honour is irrelevant when profits and success are the driving factors, and making as much profit for oneself is prized more highly than being of honourable standing.

Very many wealthy people are generally comfortable with being thought of as shitty people because well, they won at the game right? They have more commercial tokens than the other guy so that's a win isn't it?

Money-people find out the hard way that when you're on the last lap and need a bit of TLC before you check out…. money is lousy at cuddling!

The credit file is a record used by the commercial world via the agencies that maintain them, to reference everything about our 'capacity' prior to engaging in certain types of business with predominantly a financial nature. If the credit report says no - it's almost certainly a deal breaker for any commercial activity regarding finances.

The problem, when it comes to applying law to sorting out the alleged good-faith financial transaction with the bank, is that they use our credit file as a weapon against us when we call them out on their not-so-legal activities.

The judgments and defaults are a way of harming us in the future. "If you persist in 'defaulting' on our agreement and questioning our activities, then we'll cause you major problems moving forwards". Yes, that's very upstanding and hugely professional behaviour.

They create a time-bomb for our future selves whenever we need to operate in commerce again. And with more and more areas of business accessing our credit file when making decisions on whether or not to enter relations with us, it really could become severely restrictive across all areas of our lives. The credit file used to be reserved for loans and credit cards but has grown into much more lately. Rental housing, car leasing, even mobile phone contractors refer to our file, and it will only get worse in the coming years unless we correct things now.

So the bank damages our rating instead of engaging with us to deal with our concerns - because then they don't have to admit to their ancient practice of scamming their customer base. It isn't even a second thought. Their confidence in beating us down has become an accepted method for dealing with the situation to the point where they've installed automatic systems to fire out default notices as soon as two payments are missed – regardless of the reason and in absolute ignorance of our attempts to correct the matter.

The defaulting process is now done in the total absence of due cause and without any legal authority to do so.

Data Protection Act

The Data Protection Act applies to any individual or organisation that processes personal data in the UK. Other countries have equivalent Acts, legislation and codes etc.

Personal data is defined as 'any information that can be used to identify a living person, including their name, address, email address, date of birth, and other sensitive information such as medical records or financial details'.

(Interesting that persons have been defined as living entities whilst simultaneously being defined at law as a legal fiction, dead entity, corp(se)oration).

So the Data Protection Act sets out a number of principles that organisations must follow when processing personal data, including:

1. Fair and lawful processing:
   Organisations must obtain consent from

individuals to process their personal data and must only collect and use data for specific, lawful purposes.

2. Data minimisation:
   Organisations must only collect the minimum amount of personal data necessary for a particular purpose and must ensure that the data is accurate and up-to-date.

3. Purpose limitation:
   Personal data must be used only for the purposes for which it was collected and must not be used for any other purposes without the individual's consent.

4. Data retention:
   Personal data must be kept for no longer than necessary for the purposes for which it was collected.

5. Data security:
   Organisations must take appropriate measures to keep personal data secure, including protecting it from unauthorised access, loss, or damage.

The DPA also gives us certain rights in relation to our personal data, including the right to access the data held, the right to have inaccurate data corrected, and the right to have our data erased in certain circumstances.

Organisations that fail to comply with the DPA can be fined by the Information Commissioner's Office (ICO), who is responsible for enforcing the Act.

The maximum fine for a serious breach of the DPA is currently £17.5 million, or 4% of the organisation's global turnover, whichever is higher; so as you might imagine at this stage, it's a reasonably sized 'big stick' to wield.

When the bank shares our sensitive financial & personal information to third party debt collection agencies, they do so because they believe there's a legally binding contract between them and us, where we agreed to let them use, retain, and share it. That would be reasonable were the contract valid, but unfortunately, that contract – if it ever existed, has now been utterly voided by their actions to date, so it doesn't and couldn't exist.

From the point of our leaving the bank or closing the browser after the application has been made, their failures to adhere to well-established contracting rules render the entire agreement void. Everything that happens from the point of our exit is breach after breach of the very legislation implemented to restrict exactly this kind of behaviour and protect us. The conclusion of this is that they simply do not have *any* legal authority to hold, manipulate or disseminate our personal data, precisely because they cannot ever produce a valid document that states they have.

So because the bank has no contract with us, the fact that they even hold our personal data, let alone disseminate it to 3rd parties is the breach of all breaches and breaks every principle contained within the DPA.

At this stage it should be abundantly clear to anyone that we have a cause of action against the bank for its many failings and outright criminal activities regarding our relationship with them and their subsequent actions towards us.

There actually was *always* a cause of action, but prior to the research for this book, it was an uphill task to pull together all of the separate, though very much connected facets of their wrongdoings together and figure out exactly *how* to extract our remedy. The method has now been determined and uses current legislation, contract and common law, and basic common sense and fair play.

Chapter Two

Contract

The bank, from the positions below the executive level, absolutely believes that a contract exists between us and them. They won't budge on that at all, and they're happy to print off a copy of the agreement to show us.

The problem with that document is the shortcomings of the particulars of that 'agreement' in that the rules governing the formation of bona fide contracting, that have been universally settled and agreed upon, have been almost entirely abandoned. Using the rules of contract formation we can pick apart practically any modern contract for the same reason – failure to adhere to the rules of the process.

Everything the bank does, arises out of their faith that the contract is legit. As far as the executive level is concerned, they know full well that the contract doesn't exist and is precisely why they will avoid the courts to attempt to enforce something fictional.

But let's stay with the day-to-day activities of the bank's operations – specifically their insistence that we must make a payment to stay within the boundaries of the agreement. Adherence to the contract is the only defence they can cite for their actions with regard to us, but unfortunately their failures are now coming home to roost as it can easily be demonstrated that the contract they cling to was never actually legally launched. It doesn't exist and *never* existed legally, and that's because no part of their 'honest intentions' were in fact, honest.

In the realm of contract law, all parties involved are required to act in good faith and with fair dealing in mind. They're also required to meet very specific requirements in order for the contract to be legally binding upon the parties. If one party fails to adhere to the rules and then proceeds to use the imaginary agreement as a basis for making demands, issuing threats, and engaging in bad behaviour, they will likely face significant legal repercussions once the truth is discovered.

Under the rules, and assuming the contract was valid from the start, a contract is a contract and no amount of squirming can correct, produce a new component, or remove a settled component that was agreed at the outset.

A significant rule is the set-in-stone nature of the agreement. What was agreed upon at the outset is exactly what the contract determines, nothing more and nothing less, and there's a common practice in recent times that you may have noticed, *especially* with banking, where they inform us that they've made 'important changes to the agreement'.

This is forbidden under the rules and is known as *ultra vires* – beyond the contract, or outside of its scope. No one can alter the agreement once it has been signed off by the parties as that could lead to all kinds of shenanigans and cause harm to the other parties. If everyone within the agreement were free to do what they wanted under the contract, it would render the entire need for an agreement pointless.

When the banks or anyone under contract modifies the agreement in any way, the entire contract becomes void under breach conditions. With that in mind, a cursory look through emails and letters from the bank where they advise us of changes to the agreement will yield a significant harvest in terms of their breaches.

Imaginary Contract

Using an imaginary contract as if it were genuine is just incredibly stupid and leaves the door wide open to severe consequences. While an imaginary contract has no legal enforceability in itself, as we have seen when the bank routinely fails to assert its position through the courts and subsequently engages the debt collector to recover its 'losses', the actions arising from a party acting as though there is a bona fide agreement in place, are fraudulent.

Deliberate misuse of the process to induce someone to perform as though they were under a legal obligation to do so, can create all sorts of situations that won't bode well for those engaging in such action once caught.

Misrepresentation and Fraud

Using an imaginary contract as if it were genuine will likely lead to claims of misrepresentation and fraud. Misrepresentation occurs when a party makes a false statement of fact, induces the other party to rely on that statement, and causes them harm as a result. Fraud involves intentional misrepresentation with the intent to deceive.

Legislation:
Various jurisdictions have legislation addressing misrepresentation and fraud, such as the Misrepresentation Act 1967 in the United Kingdom or the Restatement (Second) of Contracts in the United States.

Case law:
In Derry v Peek (1889), the House of Lords held that a party making false statements with knowledge of their falsity or reckless disregard for the truth may be liable for a charge of fraudulent misrepresentation.

Edgington v Fitzmaurice (1885) established that if a party makes statements with the intent to deceive and induce the other party to act, they may be liable for

66

fraudulent misrepresentation.

Intimidation and Harassment

If the use of an imaginary contract involves threats, demands, or bad behaviour that amount to intimidation or harassment, the offending party may face legal consequences under anti-harassment and/or criminal laws.

Unjust Enrichment and Quantum Meruit

If the party using an imaginary contract receives a benefit from their actions or the other party provides services or goods based on the false premise, the principles of unjust enrichment and quantum meruit may come into play.

Legislation:
Jurisdictions have legal principles governing unjust enrichment and quantum meruit, such as the Restitution Act in Germany or the Restatement (Third) of Restitution and Unjust Enrichment in the United States.

Case law:
In Fibrosa Spolka Akcyjna v Fairbairn Lawson Combe Barbour Ltd (1943), the House of Lords held that if a contract is found to be illegal or unenforceable, the party who received a benefit must make restitution to the other party. Similarly, in quantum meruit, claims

arise when one party has provided goods or services with a reasonable expectation of payment, even in the absence of a formal contract.

The case of Kleinwort Benson Ltd v Lincoln City Council (1998) established that a party may be entitled to payment under a quantum meruit claim if they have provided valuable services or goods based on a mistaken belief in the existence of a contract.

Damages and Remedies

The party using an imaginary contract may also be liable for damages and other remedies based on the harm caused by their actions. Depending on the specific circumstances, the injured party can seek various forms of relief, including compensatory damages, punitive damages, injunctions, or specific performance.

Legislation governing damages and remedies varies among jurisdictions, such as the Law Reform (Miscellaneous Provisions) Act 1970 in the United Kingdom or the Uniform Commercial Code in the United States.

Case law:
In Hadley v Baxendale (1854), the court established the principles for determining the recoverability of damages in contract cases.

It would seem that the legislation is clear that using an imaginary contract as a basis for demands, threats, and bad behaviour can have severe legal repercussions for the party responsible. Misrepresentation, fraud, intimidation and harassment, unjust enrichment, and quantum meruit are just a few of the potential legal charges that could arise.

The consequences are defined by legislation and case law, and emphasise the importance of honesty, good faith, and fair dealing in contractual relationships.

Quantum meruit

This is a Latin term that translates to "as much as he has deserved" or "as much as is deserved." In legal terms it refers to a principle that allows a person to receive reasonable compensation for goods or services they have provided, even in the absence of a formal contract or agreement specifying the amount of compensation.

Quantum meruit is often invoked in situations where there is an implied or quasi-contractual relationship between parties, meaning that there's an understanding or expectation that payment will be made for the goods or services rendered. It arises when one party has provided valuable services, materials, or labor to another party, but there is no express contract specifying the terms of payment.

When a dispute arises regarding the amount of compensation owed, the court can use the principle of quantum meruit to determine a fair and reasonable amount. The court will consider various factors such as the nature and value of the services provided, prevailing industry rates, and any relevant circumstances or agreements between the parties. Quantum meruit is commonly applied in areas such as construction, professional services, and other situations where the parties involved may not have entered into a formal contract but have still received and benefitted from goods or services. It serves as a legal recourse to prevent unjust enrichment, ensuring that individuals or businesses that have provided valuable contributions are fairly compensated for their efforts, even in the absence of a written agreement.

Quasi-Contract

A quasi-contract is a fictional contract recognised by a court. The notion of a quasi-contract can be traced to Roman law and is still a concept used in some modern legal systems. Quasi contract laws have been deduced from the Latin statement "Nemo debet locupletari ex aliena jactura", which proclaims that no man should grow rich out of another person's loss. It was one of the central doctrines of Roman law.

Chapter Three

Bank Transparency

The Economic Crime (Transparency and Enforcement) Act 2022 is legislation aimed at addressing economic crimes and improving transparency and enforcement in financial transactions.

The Act introduced measures to combat money laundering, corruption, fraud, and other illicit activities.

Key provisions include:

1. Enhanced reporting requirements:
   The Act imposes stricter reporting obligations on financial institutions and businesses, requiring them to disclose suspicious transactions and implement robust anti-money laundering measures.

2. Strengthened enforcement powers:
   Additional powers were granted to law
   enforcement agencies and regulatory bodies to
   investigate economic crimes, seize assets, and
   prosecute offenders more effectively.

3. Whistleblower protection:
   The Act introduced provisions to protect
   whistleblowers that report economic crimes,
   encouraging individuals to come forward with
   valuable information without fear of retaliation.

4. Cross-border cooperation:
   The Act emphasises international cooperation in
   combatting economic crimes by promoting
   information sharing and coordination among
   different jurisdictions.

5. Asset recovery and confiscation:
   The Act enhances mechanisms for the recovery
   and confiscation of assets derived from economic
   crimes, aiming to deprive criminals of their ill-
   gotten gains.

This chapter may seem unrelated at first glance
primarily because the Act seems to ignore the elephant
in the living room, but there are elements within it that
can be used in our claim to the bank.

The overarching aim of the Act was to make the banks
(in particular) more readily reviewable, and to
implement tighter measures for the reporting and
managing of their business. It gives them more powers

to investigate and implement action on those that would enrich themselves through ill-gotten gains.

What it fails to do is address the foundational problem that is, that the basis for modern banking activity is to relieve US of our hard-earned cash through questionable activities.

The Act undoubtedly came about due to pressure to restrain the banker's penchant for involving themselves in deals that were less than fair and legal – and because the civil service had to demonstrate to the public (at least on paper) that the banks were still under the control of government.

This was all obviously in addition to providing some (vacuous) satisfaction to the Parliamentary flock that 'something' had been done. The (paper exercise) Act did however, provide a way for us to demand that the bank stands accountable to some degree for their actions – at least on the face of it, via citing the new legislation and the requirement under law for them to cease being secretive.

It doesn't work in practice however, as they *always* claim (purely coincidentally of course) that the exact data we're looking for is private and 'commercially sensitive' information.

Quite how MY account information could be THEIR private and sensitive information is beyond me, but there it is. What they really mean is that the notes and comments they add to the account details are what they don't want us to see, because that would reveal details about their dodgy operations. It's just another tell about what they're really up to behind the curtain, and we still can't force them to produce their ledger.

This can all be used against them though as we'll see later.

Chapter Four

Misrepresentation

The Misrepresentation Act 1967 is a piece of legislation that's been in operation in the United Kingdom for over half a century and has its counterparts across the world. It sets out the legal framework for dealing with misrepresentations made in the context of commercial transactions, and provides remedies for those who have been misled or deceived as a result.

Misrepresentation occurs when a false statement is made, either intentionally or unintentionally, that induces someone to enter into a contract or transaction. The Act provides legal remedy for those who suffer financial loss as a result of such misrepresentations.

The Act applies to misrepresentations made before or at the time of contract / agreement formation, and also to statements made during negotiations leading up to the contract.

It covers both innocent and fraudulent misrepresentation, as well as negligent misrepresentation.

An innocent misrepresentation is one where the person making the statement genuinely believes it to be true, but it turns out to be false.

A fraudulent misrepresentation is one where the person making the statement knows it to be false or is 'economical' as to its truth.

A negligent misrepresentation is one where the person making the statement does not take reasonable care to ensure its accuracy.

Under the Act, a misrepresentation claim is possible if it is a material factor in inducing the other party to enter into the contract. This means, that the misrepresentation must be an important consideration that led the other party to make the decision to enter into the contract.

If a misrepresentation claim is used, the innocent party has several remedies available to them. They may rescind the contract, meaning they can cancel the agreement and seek a return to the position they were in before the contract was made, or alternatively, they may seek damages for any financial loss they have suffered as a result of the misrepresentation.

In order to rescind the contract, the innocent party must act promptly once they become aware of the misrepresentation. If they delay in taking action, they may be deemed to have accepted the contract and lose their right to rescind.

The Act also sets out a number of defences that may be used by the person who made the misrepresentation. These include showing that the misrepresentation was not made fraudulently or negligently, or that the innocent party had the opportunity to investigate the situation but failed to do so. Although, when dealing with banks, we always give them plenty of opportunity to correct the record and they subsequently *always* maintain a hard pass to respond appropriately.

It's crucial for both parties entering into a commercial transaction to take care when making statements and to ensure that they are accurate and truthful. Failing to do so can result in significant financial and legal consequences, as well as damage to reputation and relationships.

With regard to the alleged agreement we entered into with the bank, there's hardly a part of what they said that stands as true. Their entire pitch was misrepresentation!

1. Misrepresenting their intent

2. Failure to produce consideration

3. Failure to disclose that we created a security instrument

4. Failure to disclose that they insured the account against us

5. Failure to inform us that we created the credit

6. Failure to disclose that they sell our instrument on the markets

7. Failure to disburse profits gained from trading our property

8. Failure to halt automated reporting processes

9. Failure to respond appropriately

10. Failure to sign off documentation under required legislation.

All of this combines to produce a spectacular flouting of the legislation that was designed specifically to govern their activities.

When the piper comes calling on the banks they'll have a very difficult time in defending their actions during our business with them. They have zero standing in the matter and cannot evidence a bona fide contract between the parties, therefore, everything they have done, said, and believe to be true, is without legal basis.

Chapter Five

Defamation

The Defamation Act 2013 was passed by UK Parliament to reform the legal framework for defamation claims. It was enacted on January 1, 2014, and replaced the previous Act, which was seen as outdated and overly restrictive.

The Act introduced several significant changes to the legislation, including:

1. A new test for determining whether a statement is defamatory

2. A requirement for claimants to show that they have suffered serious harm before bringing a claim

3. A defence of 'honest opinion' that replaced the

old defence of 'fair comment'.

Under the old version, a statement was considered defamatory if it tended to lower the claimant in the estimation of right-thinking members of society. That position was seen as too subjective and resulted in many claims being brought into the court based on trivial or insignificant matters.

The new test (set out in section 1 of the Act) provides that a statement is defamatory if it "causes or is likely to cause serious harm to the reputation of the claimant." This test is more objective and focuses on the actual harm caused by the statement rather than the subjective perceptions of society.

Another important change brought about is the requirement for claimants to show that they have suffered serious harm before bringing a claim. This is intended to prevent trivial claims being brought.

Serious harm is defined as harm that is "serious enough to warrant an action for damages without proof of special damage."

Under the previous legislation, the defence of fair comment applied to statements of opinion on matters of public interest. The defence required that the comment be based on true facts, be honestly held, and be made without malice.

The new defence of honest opinion (set out in section 3 of the Act) applies to statements of opinion on any matter. The defence requires that the opinion be based on true facts that were either stated or readily available, that the opinion be honestly held, and that it was a matter of public interest to express the opinion.

Also introduced was a new defence of "publication on a matter of public interest." This defence (set out in section 4), provides that a defendant is not liable for defamation if they can show that the statement was published on a matter of public interest and that they reasonably believed that publishing the statement was in the public interest.

The Act also made some changes to the procedures for bringing and defending defamation claims. For example, it introduced a new "single publication rule" which is a limitation on the time period for bringing claims in respect of publications that are available online. Under the new rule, a claim must be brought within one year of the first publication of the statement.

In addition, the Act provides for process of early resolution of defamation disputes, known as the "offer of amends" procedure. Under this, a defendant who has made a defamatory statement can make an offer of amends to the claimant, which if accepted, can lead to a resolution of the dispute without the need for court proceedings.

Overall, the Defamation Act 2013 represents a significant reform of the legislation for defamation in the UK. Its provisions are designed to strike a better balance between protecting reputations, promoting free speech, and prevent trivial claims from clogging up the courts.

While the Act has drawn a fair amount of controversy, particularly in relation to the new serious harm test, it is generally seen as a positive development.

That the bank make negative judgments onto our credit file, is a tort on our position; a sullying of our reputation and a slur on our good name. In the grand scheme of things the bank has no legal right to do this a) because we flagged the many issues we have, as being of severe importance, and their only response was to deliberately injure our status, and b) because no actual contract between us exists.

So the bank attacked our commercial vehicle rather than engage in answering awkward questions. This discrediting of our commercial reputation, including a brief description they write in the report (that's shown on our file) is not just incorrect - because how can we default on an imaginary loan or credit facility when it can be shown positively that there is no such agreement in place for which they can claim a breach? It is also defamation under the section 'serious harm', because it directly impacts our commercial functionality and psychological well-being.

Nothing they say in their report is true and the absolute best it could be, is yet another mistake on their part. They assume there is a contract in place and that we breached it. All of that is demonstrably incorrect, as they made no attempt to investigate our claims and attacked us without due cause or any legal basis to do so. They might claim innocence in their actions, but we can easily and positively demonstrate our efforts to co-operate via the attempts we made to resolve the matter via our correspondence with them - that they subsequently declined to respond appropriately to. At that point their defence of innocence will fail.

Defamation is the soft name for it, but actually in this instance, it is criminal damage.

Chapter Six

Unjust Enrichment

Unjust enrichment is a legal concept that has its roots in common law. It's a principle that operates in situations where one party has received a benefit at the expense of another party without any legal justification.

Unjust enrichment seeks to remedy the situation by requiring the party that has received the benefit, to make restitution to the party that has suffered the loss.

The concept is recognised and applied by courts in the United States, Canada, Australia, and the United Kingdom.

Historical Development of Unjust Enrichment

The concept is rooted in Roman law where the Roman jurist Gaius recognised the principle, stating, "no one should be unjustly enriched at the expense of another." It wasn't given much attention at the time and wasn't until the 19th century that it began to gain traction in common law jurisdictions.

In England, the principle was first recognised in the 17th century in the case of Moses v Macferlan (1760) 2 Burr 1005. Macferlan had been paid by Moses to sell some stock on his behalf but Macferlan did not sell the stock and instead used the money for his own purposes. Moses sued Macferlan for the return of the money, and the court held that Macferlan had been unjustly enriched at Moses' expense and ordered him to make restitution.

In the 20th century, the principle was developed further in a series of cases in the United Kingdom, including Lipkin Gorman v Karpnale (1991) 2 AC 548 and Westdeutsche Landesbank v Islington LBC (1996) AC 669. These cases clarified the principles of unjust enrichment and established a framework for analysis.

There then came a standard by which to define the principle.

Principles of Unjust Enrichment

1. A party must have been enriched. The first requirement for a claim of unjust enrichment is that the defendant must have been enriched. Enrichment can take many forms, including the receipt of money, goods, or services.

2. The enrichment must have been at the expense of the claimant. This means that the claimant must have suffered a loss as a result of the enrichment.

3. There must be no legal justification for the enrichment. The defendant must not have received the enrichment as a result of a valid contract, a legal obligation, or a statutory provision.

4. Restitution must be possible. This means that the defendant must be able to make restitution to the claimant, either by returning the enrichment or by paying compensation for the loss suffered by the claimant.

Application of Unjust Enrichment

Unjust enrichment can be applied in a variety of contexts, including contract law, tort law, and property law. In each of these areas, unjust enrichment operates to prevent one party from receiving a benefit at the expense of another party without legal justification.

Under Contract Law

In contract law, unjust enrichment operates as a remedy when there is no valid contract between the parties. For example, if A pays B to deliver goods to C, but B fails to deliver the goods and keeps the money, A may have a claim for unjust enrichment against B. This is because B has been enriched at A's expense without any legal justification. In such a situation, A may seek restitution from B for the money paid.

Unjust enrichment can also be used to supplement the terms of a contract where the contract is silent on a particular issue. For instance, if A and B enter into a contract for the sale of a car, and the contract is silent on who bears the risk of loss if the car is damaged during transit, unjust enrichment may operate to determine who should bear the loss. In such a situation, the party who has been enriched at the expense of the other party may be required to make restitution.

Under Tort Law

In tort law, the principle may arise in situations for instance, if a defendant negligently causes damage to the property of the claimant, the defendant may have been enriched at the claimant's expense because the defendant has received a benefit (avoiding the cost of repairing the damage) without any legal justification. The claimant may, therefore, seek restitution for the loss suffered.

Under Property Law

In property law, unjust enrichment may arise in situations where a person has acquired property at the expense of another person without any legal justification. For example, if A mistakenly pays B for property that B does not own, and B keeps the money, A may have a claim for unjust enrichment against B. This is because B has been enriched at A's expense without any legal justification. A may, therefore, seek restitution from B for the money paid.

In other words, unjust enrichment occurs when someone gains an unfair advantage or benefit from another person's loss or disadvantage. The principle is a foundational concept in the law of restitution, which is concerned with the recovery of benefits conferred by one party on another. In order to establish a claim, the claimant must prove three elements: enrichment, impoverishment, and absence of legal basis.

Impoverishment can take many forms, such as the loss of money, property, or services. It can also arise from the assumption of a liability, such as a debt or an obligation to pay for goods or services. The key is that the claimant must have suffered a loss or disadvantage as a result of the defendant's enrichment.

The absence of legal basis means that there is no legal justification for the defendant's enrichment. This can arise in various ways, such as where the defendant has received the benefit by mistake, fraud, duress, or undue influence. It can also arise where the defendant has received the benefit as a result of a breach of trust or fiduciary duty.

Types of Enrichment

There are several different types of enrichment that can give rise to a claim in restitution:

1. Direct enrichment: This occurs where the defendant has received a benefit directly from the claimant, such as the payment of money or the provision of services.

2. Indirect enrichment: This occurs where the defendant has received a benefit indirectly from the claimant, such as the payment of money to a third party on the defendant's behalf.

3. Mistaken payment: This occurs where the claimant has paid the defendant by mistake, such

as where the claimant believed that the defendant was entitled to the payment when in fact he or she was not.

4. Failure of consideration: This occurs where the defendant has received payment for goods or services that were not delivered or were delivered in a defective or unsatisfactory condition.

5. Breach of contract: This occurs where the defendant has breached a contract with the claimant, such as by failing to perform the agreed-upon services or by delivering defective goods.

6. Restitution for wrongs: This occurs where the defendant has committed a wrong against the claimant, such as fraud, duress, undue influence, or breach of trust or fiduciary duty.

Defenses to Unjust Enrichment

There are several defences that can be raised against a claim of unjust enrichment. These include:

1. Change of position: This occurs where the defendant has spent or disposed of the benefit received in good faith and in such a way that it would be unjust to require him or her to repay it.

2. Statutory bar: This occurs where a statute provides that a claim for restitution cannot be brought in certain circumstances.

3. Limitation period: This occurs where the claim is barred by the applicable limitation period.

4. Consent: This occurs where the claimant has consented to the defendant's enrichment, either expressly or impliedly.

5. Illegality: This occurs where the enrichment is the result of an illegal transaction, such as a contract to commit a crime.

Remedies for Unjust Enrichment

If a claimant succeeds in establishing a claim for unjust enrichment, he or she may be entitled to a range of remedies. These include:

1. Restitution: This involves the return of the benefit received by the defendant to the claimant.

2. Damages: This involves compensation for the loss or damage suffered by the claimant as a result of the defendant's enrichment.

3. Account of profits: This involves the payment to the claimant of the profits earned by the defendant as a result of the enrichment.

4. Constructive trust: This involves the imposition of a trust over the property or assets in question, with the defendant holding them on behalf of the claimant.

Chapter Seven

Financial Services Act

The Bank of England and Financial Services Act 2016 is UK legislation that aims to reform the financial services industry and strengthen the regulatory powers of the Bank of England. The Act was passed in response to the 2008 financial crisis, which highlighted the need for greater oversight and regulation of the financial services industry. Strangely, it failed to state that the Bank of England is a private corporation owned and operated by unknown individuals for personal gain.

Foxes guarding the Chickens?

The Act is divided into six parts, each of which focuses on a different aspect of financial regulation.

Part 1 establishes the Prudential Regulation Authority (PRA) as a subsidiary of the Bank of England with responsibility for regulating and supervising banks, building societies, and other financial institutions. The PRA is tasked with ensuring that these institutions are financially stable and able to withstand economic shocks.

So basically, a private financial establishment (The Bank of England) gives *itself* the ability to regulate every other private financial establishment?

Part 2 of the Act establishes the Financial Policy Committee (FPC), which is also a subsidiary of the Bank of England, and is responsible for identifying and responding to risks to the stability of the financial system as a whole. The FPC has the power to recommend actions to the PRA and other regulatory bodies in order to mitigate these risks.

Again, that same private financial establishment gives itself a different set of abilities to regulate every other private financial establishment.

Part 3 of the Act establishes the Financial Conduct Authority (FCA), which is responsible for regulating and supervising financial markets and protecting consumers. The FCA is tasked with ensuring that financial products and services are fair, transparent, and accessible to consumers, and has the power to take enforcement action against firms that breach its rules.

This one is slightly better concealed. However, after digging we learn that the FCA is funded by the banks; those same banks that are all regulated by the Bank of England.

So the FCA investigates all of the banks that pay their wages. How then, do we think their objectivity will play out in terms of them calling out and applying sanctions against their paymaster?

Part 4 of the Act makes a number of amendments to the regulatory regime for insurance companies, including the establishment of a new regulatory framework for the management of insurance companies in distress.

They would be the same insurance companies that underwrite the bank's imaginary losses I'd guess.

Part 5 of the Act contains miscellaneous provisions, including amendments to the Bank of England Act 1998 and the Financial Services and Markets Act 2000. These amendments are intended to strengthen the *regulatory powers* of the Bank of England and other regulatory bodies, and to improve the functioning of the financial services industry as a whole.

Again, all controlled by a wealthy group of private individuals running a private institution for profit and masquerading as an upstanding cornerstone of this and every other country. (And don't think the Federal Reserve is any different!)

Finally, Part 6 of the Act contains provisions relating to the regulation of the payment systems industry. This part of the Act is intended to ensure that payment systems are secure, efficient, and reliable, and that they operate in a competitive environment.

And all of that is in addition to them regulating the bejesus out of ALL of the so-called competition.

It seems that all this Act has achieved is a greater ability for the banks to extract our money, while simultaneously basking in an environment of a reduced requirement for accountability, and for anyone to have recourse against them. Can we say *cartel* at this point?

Since the Act was passed, there have been a number of high-profile cases in which the PRA, FPC, and FCA have taken enforcement action against financial institutions that have breached their rules. For example, in 2017 the FCA fined Barclays Bank £72 million for failing to manage conflicts of interest in relation to a £1.9 billion fundraising deal.

In 2018, the PRA fined Goldman Sachs International £34 million for failing to provide accurate and timely reporting of its capital position.

Despite these enforcement actions however, there are still concerns among bankers that the UK financial services industry is not sufficiently regulated. In particular, there are concerns that the regulatory regime for the fintech industry is not adequate, and that the rapid growth of fintech firms could pose a risk to financial stability.

Fintech is the composite term for financial / technology companies, where we can see that they want to sew up any potential for someone to create a truly independent digital currency system that isn't specifically approved (and 100% controlled) by them.

There are also concerns that the UK's departure from the European Union could lead to a weakening of the regulatory framework, as the UK will no longer be subject to EU regulations and directives.

This Act is ALL showboating. It had to be demonstrated that their creation had an effect and *any* effect would work, to draw attention away from it being yet another step towards cementing the monopoly banking situation.

One potential area for improvement is in the coordination between the different regulatory bodies. The Act created three distinct bodies with overlapping responsibilities, and it's important to this stitch-up that they all work together effectively to ensure that the regulatory framework is coherent and consistent.

There are also concerns that there may be gaps in regulation, particularly in relation to emerging risks such as cyber threats and climate change. Addressing these issues will require ongoing collaboration and dialogue between industry stakeholders and regulatory bodies to combat any potential threats, such as tech geeks sweating over their computers to figure out new ways of poking holes in the bankers' precious system.

How can any doubt remain that those three regulatory bodies are *not* already in symphony together? They were all created by the same master to perform the same (ultimate) function.

Overall, the Bank of England and Financial Services Act 2016 represents an important milestone in the regulation of the UK financial services industry by giving even more power to the Bank of England. The bottom line (as always) is that the banks are increasingly restricting any potential for regulation - except by themselves. They have very little by way of accountability to the people - only to their self-created (and ultimately subservient) theatre of 'control'.

Chapter Eight
Modern Slavery Act

The Modern Slavery Act 2015 is aimed at combating the issue of modern slavery in the UK. The Act consolidates existing offences of slavery and human trafficking, and introduces new measures to prevent and punish these crimes.

The Act defines modern slavery as encompassing a range of exploitative practices, including forced labour, debt bondage, human trafficking, and actual slavery. It also acknowledges that modern slavery can take many forms, including sexual exploitation, forced begging, and organ harvesting.

One of the key provisions of the Act is the requirement for companies with a turnover of £36m or more to publish an annual statement outlining the steps they have taken to prevent modern slavery in their supply chains. This statement must be approved by the board of directors and made publicly available. So right out of the gate there's potential for shenanigans as this would be the board of directors of the same company.

The Act also introduces tougher penalties for those convicted of modern slavery offences and offenders can face life imprisonment for the most serious crimes, such as trafficking and slavery. The maximum sentence for other offences has been increased to 14 years.

Another important aspect is the provision of new powers for law enforcement agencies to tackle the problem. This includes the power to seize assets believed to be the proceeds of modern slavery, and the power to obtain slavery and trafficking prevention orders to restrict the activities of suspected offenders.

The Act also provides protection for victims, including the creation of a statutory defence for those who have been forced to commit crimes. This defence recognises that victims of modern slavery are often coerced into criminal activities, and seeks to ensure that they are not further victimised by the criminal justice system.

In addition, the Act establishes the role of the Independent Anti-Slavery Commissioner, whose remit is to promote best practice in the prevention of modern slavery and the identification and support of victims.

Since its introduction in 2015, the Act has had a significant impact on efforts to combat modern slavery in the UK. The requirement for companies to publish statements on their efforts to prevent modern slavery in their supply chains has led to increased awareness of the issue among businesses and consumers, and has encouraged greater accountability and transparency in supply chains.

There has been criticism of the Act, particularly in relation to its effectiveness in preventing and prosecuting modern slavery offences.

Some campaigners argue that the Act does not go far enough in terms of protecting victims and preventing modern slavery, and that more needs to be done to ensure that those responsible for these crimes are brought to justice.

Now slavery, on the face of it would seem an unlikely category to include in this work, but in reality, when we are first duped by deceptive practice and lead to believe that what we entered was above-board and legit, the actions that flow *from* that alleged contract have a direct impact on our financial situation for many years, all while we believe that we're legitimately compelled into performance under a bona fide contract.

The pseudo-contracting process lead us to an imposition whereby we feel obligated to endure it - sometimes for years. It reinforced the belief that there's a legally binding *requirement* on our part to service the account - or face the consequences.

That imposition is actually slavery by definition. We feel obligated to continually pay to service an imaginary debt, to an imaginary lender, under threat of further impositions and eventual damage to our standing if we don't maintain the situation.

That situation forces most of us into labour of some description to continue earning enough money to meet the demands. That labour, wouldn't need to be performed and certainly not to the same extent, if we'd known the truth of the matter from the outset. And that particular scenario is called *debt bondage*.

Debt Bondage

Debt bondage, also known as debt slavery or bonded labour, is a form of exploitation that persists everywhere in the world. It involves individuals who are forced into servitude at some level as a result of debts that they would be otherwise unable to repay.

Debt bondage is not a new situation. Throughout history, economic and social systems have allowed individuals and even entire communities to fall into imaginary debt and become trapped in the cycle of bondage.

In its current form it evolved with the worldwide spread of economies and the exploitation of vulnerable populations where simple sleight of hand can embroil us into a potential lifetime of toiling to meet someone's imaginary claim upon our energy.

Debt bondage affects more people in Western countries than most realise and that's primarily because it's very difficult to see when covered over by legislation. It's a simple premise; if you must labour to generate money to pay a debt, and that debt cannot or will not be validated then a) the debt is fake and b) you are in debt bondage.

Debt bondage is actually a violation of human rights, as it deprives individuals of their fundamental freedoms, dignity, and autonomy. Criminal networks exploit the vulnerabilities of individuals, for example; our perfectly natural and normal ignorance of the secretive intricacies of banking practice, that are daily used against us to perpetuate a nearly impossible-to-break descent into privation and eventual poverty.

Legislation exists to protect us, but we have to know how to wield it – and that's assuming we're even aware of it.

Debt bondage is a relatively simple concept to prove out once we know the facts, and that, as always, begins with the contract-that-doesn't-exist.

Chapter Nine

Fraud

Fraud comprises all acts or omissions or concealments involving breach of equitable or legal duty or trust or confidence.

The Fraud Act 2006 makes provision for, and in connection with, criminal liability for fraud and obtaining services dishonestly. It's an act of the UK Parliament that criminalises various types of fraudulent activities and consists of three main offences, which are:

1. Fraud by false representation

2. Fraud by failing to disclose information

3. Fraud by abuse of position

The Act also includes provisions on conspiracy to commit fraud and offences related to obtaining services dishonestly.

Fraud by false representation

This is defined as "dishonestly making a false representation with the intention of causing a gain or loss to another person". It covers a wide range of activities, such as making false claims for insurance, selling counterfeit goods, and making false statements in financial documents. To be convicted, the prosecutor must prove that the defendant made a false representation; that the defendant knew the representation was false; and that the representation was made with the intention of causing a gain or loss.

Fraud by failing to disclose information

This is defined as "dishonestly failing to disclose information that the defendant has a legal duty to disclose, and with the intention of causing a gain or loss to another person". It covers situations where a person fails to disclose information that would affect the decision of another person, such as a company director failing to disclose a conflict of interest.

To be convicted under the Fraud Act, the prosecutor must prove that the defendant had a legal duty to disclose the information, that the defendant knew of the duty to disclose, and that the defendant failed to disclose the information with the intention of causing a gain or loss.

Fraud by abuse of position

This is defined as "dishonestly abusing a position of trust or responsibility in order to make a gain or cause a loss to another person". It covers situations where a person in a position of trust, such as a company director or a public official, uses their position for personal gain.

To be convicted, the prosecutor must prove that the defendant was in a position of trust or responsibility, that the defendant abused that position, and that the abuse was dishonest and intended to cause a gain or loss.

The Act also includes provisions on conspiracy to commit fraud, such as situations where two or more people agree to commit a fraudulent activity, even if the activity is not actually carried out.

To be convicted of this offence, the prosecutor must prove that the defendant agreed with others to commit a fraudulent activity, that the defendant intended to carry out the activity, and that at least one act was taken towards carrying out the activity.

Also included in the Act are offences relating to obtaining services dishonestly and covers situations where a person obtains services dishonestly, such as by using a stolen credit card or by pretending to be someone else.

To be convicted, the prosecutor must prove that the defendant obtained services dishonestly, that the defendant knew they were obtaining services dishonestly, and that the services obtained had a value of more than £11,000.

Fraud can be applied to any financial crime that involves deception, misrepresentation, or false statements, such as securities fraud, tax fraud, or wire fraud.

Relevant sections of the Act

1. Fraud

(1) A person is guilty of fraud if he is in breach of any of the sections listed in subsection (2) (which provide for different ways of committing the offence).

(2) The sections are —

(a) section 2 (fraud by false representation),

(b) section 3 (fraud by failing to disclose information), and

(c) section 4 (fraud by abuse of position).

(3) A person who is guilty of fraud is liable —

(a) on summary conviction, to imprisonment for a term not exceeding [F1 the general limit in a magistrates' court] or to a fine not exceeding the statutory maximum (or to both);

(b) on conviction on indictment, to imprisonment for a term not exceeding 10 years or to a fine (or to both).

2. Fraud by false representation

(1) A person is in breach of this section if he —

(a) dishonestly makes a false representation, and

(b) intends, by making the representation —

(i) to make a gain for himself or another, or

(ii) to cause loss to another or to expose another to a risk of loss.

(2) A representation is false if —

(a) it is untrue or misleading, and

(b) the person making it knows that it is, or might be, untrue or misleading.

(3) "Representation" means any representation as to fact or law, including a representation as to the state of mind of —

(a) the person making the representation, or

(b) any other person.

(4) A representation may be express or implied.

(5) For the purposes of this section a representation may be regarded as made if it (or anything implying it) is submitted in any form to any system or device designed to receive, convey or respond to communications (with or without human intervention).

3. Fraud by failing to disclose information

A person is in breach of this section if he —

(a) dishonestly fails to disclose to another person information which he is under a legal duty to disclose, and

(b) intends, by failing to disclose the information —

(i) to make a gain for himself or another, or

(ii) to cause loss to another or to expose another to a risk of loss.

4. Fraud by abuse of position

(1) A person is in breach of this section if he—

(a) occupies a position in which he is expected to safeguard, or not to act against, the financial interests of another person,

(b) dishonestly abuses that position, and

(c) intends, by means of the abuse of that position—

(i) to make a gain for himself or another, or

(ii) to cause loss to another or to expose another to a risk of loss.

(2) A person may be regarded as having abused his position even though his conduct consisted of an omission rather than an act.

5. "Gain" and "loss"

(1) The references to gain and loss in sections 2 to 4 are to be read in accordance with this section.

(2) "Gain" and "loss" —

(a) extend only to gain or loss in money or other property;

(b) include any such gain or loss whether temporary or permanent;

and "property" means any property whether real or personal (including things in action and other intangible property).

(3) "Gain" includes a gain by keeping what one has, as well as a gain by getting what one does not have.

(4) "Loss" includes a loss by not getting what one might get, as well as a loss by parting with what one has.

6. Possession etc. of articles for use in frauds

(1) A person is guilty of an offence if he has in his possession or under his control any article for use in the course of or in connection with any fraud.

(2) A person guilty of an offence under this section is liable —

(a) on summary conviction, to imprisonment for a term not exceeding [F1 the general limit in a magistrates' court] or to a fine not exceeding the statutory maximum (or to both);

(b) on conviction on indictment, to imprisonment for a term not exceeding 5 years or to a fine (or to both).

7. Making or supplying articles for use in frauds

(1) A person is guilty of an offence if he makes, adapts, supplies or offers to supply any article —

(a) knowing that it is designed or adapted for use in the course of or in connection with fraud, or

(b) intending it to be used to commit, or assist in the commission of, fraud.

(2) A person guilty of an offence under this section is liable —

(a) on summary conviction, to imprisonment for a term not exceeding [F1 the general limit in a magistrates' court] or to a fine not exceeding the statutory maximum (or to both);

(b) on conviction on indictment, to imprisonment for a term not exceeding 10 years or to a fine (or to both).

8. "Article"

(1) For the purposes of —

(a) sections 6 and 7, and

(b) the provisions listed in subsection (2), so far as they relate to articles for use in

123

the course of or in connection with fraud,

"article" includes any program or data held in electronic form.

(2) The provisions are—

(a) section 1(7)(b) of the Police and Criminal Evidence Act 1984 (c. 60),

(b) section 2(8)(b) of the Armed Forces Act 2001 (c. 19).

11. Obtaining services dishonestly

(1) A person is guilty of an offence under this section if he obtains services for himself or another—

(a) by a dishonest act, and

(b) in breach of subsection (2).

(2) A person obtains services in breach of this subsection if—

(a) they are made available on the basis that payment has been, is being or will be made for or in respect of them,

(b) he obtains them without any payment having been made for or in respect of them or without payment having been made in full, and

(c) when he obtains them, he knows —

(i) that they are being made available on the basis described in paragraph (a), or

(ii) that they might be, but intends that payment will not be made, or will not be made in full.

(3) A person guilty of an offence under this section is liable —

(a) on summary conviction, to imprisonment for a term not exceeding [F1 the general limit in a magistrates' court] or to a fine not exceeding the statutory maximum (or to both);

(b) on conviction on indictment, to imprisonment for a term not exceeding 5 years or to a fine (or to both).

12. Liability of company officers for offences by company

(1) Subsection (2) applies if an offence under this Act is

committed by a body corporate.

(2) If the offence is proved to have been committed with the consent or connivance of —

(a) a director, manager, secretary or other similar officer of the body corporate, or

(b) a person who was purporting to act in any such capacity,

he (as well as the body corporate) is guilty of the offence and liable to be proceeded against and punished accordingly.

(3) If the affairs of a body corporate are managed by its members, subsection (2) applies in relation to the acts and defaults of a member in connection with his functions of management as if he were a director of the body corporate.

13. Evidence

(1) A person is not to be excused from —

(a) answering any question put to him in proceedings relating to property, or

(b) complying with any order made in proceedings relating to property,

on the ground that doing so may incriminate him or his spouse or civil partner of an offence under this Act or a related offence.

(2) But, in proceedings for an offence under this Act or a related offence, a statement or admission made by the person in —
(a) answering such a question, or

(b) complying with such an order,

is not admissible in evidence against him or (unless they married or became civil partners after the making of the statement or admission) his spouse or civil partner.

(3) "Proceedings relating to property" means any proceedings for —

(a) the recovery or administration of any property,

(b) the execution of a trust, or
(c) an account of any property or dealings with property,

and "property" means money or other property whether real or personal (including things in action and other intangible property).

(4) "Related offence" means —

(a) conspiracy to defraud;

(b) any other offence involving any form

of fraudulent conduct or purpose.

Sections of the Act relevant to our claim upon the bank / CC Company

Section 2

The entirety of section 2 applies in our situation as the bank have engaged in (a), (b), and (c).

(a) fraud by false representation.

The bank knowingly and deliberately expanded our belief that they were lending something to us ie. that an amount of money belonging to them was transferred from their account to ours.

They also encouraged us and expanded our belief that a genuine contract was being created between the parties and yet failed to adhere to the most basic of contracting requirements.

(b) fraud by failing to disclose information.

The bank deliberately withheld critical information such as the fact that we created a Security Instrument and handed it to them in ignorance, that they accepted it as CASH, and that they added it to their ledger as a gift / profit / salvaged or abandoned property, or free money.

That they sold our Security on the markets, kept the

profits, and failed to return the instrument upon redemption.

(b) intends, by failing to disclose the information —

(i) *to make a gain for himself or another, or*

They sold our property (the instrument), kept the profits, took our *re*payments, took interest payments, and initiated an insurance policy to cover their 'losses'.

(ii) *to cause loss to another or to expose another to a risk of loss.*

All of the above applies.

(c) fraud by abuse of position.

The bank does nothing *but* abuse their position by purporting to be a lender and stating that they can help us improve our circumstances by lending us money.

(a) *occupies a position in which he is expected to safeguard, or not to act against, the financial interests of another person,*

By acting in the way that they do, the ONLY thing the bank does is act *against* our financial position and wellbeing.

(b) *dishonestly abuses that position, and*

(c) intends, by means of the abuse of that position –

> *(i)   to make a gain for himself or another, or*
> *(ii) to cause loss to another or to expose another to a risk of loss.*

(2) A person may be regarded as having abused his position even though his conduct consisted of an omission rather than an act.

The bank's blanket policy of not fully disclosing their actual position at the contracting stage, regarding where the money came from, stealing our property and selling it for profit, is omission.

The Fraud Act 2006 covers pretty much all of what we're looking at with the bank and there's much of what they do that crosses over into other Acts that can be sub-categorised into its own areas.

An important digression here; I've said it many times and will continue to do so; every country that has a central banking system has its own rules and legislation but it is always inline with all other countries with the notable exceptions of Iran, North Korea and other 'axis of evil' territories.

You can use everything contained in this book in all jurisdictions, exceptions included, but you'll need to locate the relevant corresponding legislation where you are. It's all based on universal contract law and common sense in the end.

On the face of it, fraud would seem to be the best and most comprehensive route to go down for our claim against the bank, but here's the kicker; Claims of fraud against a bank are unlikely to succeed.
The odds stacked against registering a case against a bank for fraud and gaining any merit, are astronomical. Many have tried and most (maybe all) have failed.

So why is this?

Well, the simple answer is that claims of fraud against a bank are just not permitted – or at least that's how the situation seems to be. The court will not accept it and their reasoning isn't immediately obvious until you realise who exactly it is that pays their wages and keeps the system running.

So whilst we can build a strong case for fraud against the bank and positively prove our claims, that case is unlikely to be given merit, and the chance for progression to the court is slim to zero.

It isn't all doom & gloom though, as none of this stops us from citing the charges in our pre-action letter to the bank. It strengthens our case against them and shows that we have a solid grasp of exactly what they're up to.

Another aspect, that we shouldn't be experiencing at all, is the propensity of DCA's to use the non-court route of employing the services of (in the UK) The Civil National Business Centre in Northampton (formerly the Northampton County Court Business Centre). This is not a court and has no ability to produce a legitimate court judgment. Instead they are generating 'court

orders' by process of rubber stamping 'cases' –
sometimes thousands in a single day.

Then there's the local council who hire a room in the
local courts for a day and pretty much do their
'administration' behind closed doors.

Both of these operations are NOT legitimate courtrooms
and the subsequent 'order' is masquerading as one
issued from a bona fide court.

Because the 'order' failed on just about every aspect of
due process they don't have access to Bailiffs to enforce
the money-grab, but they do seem to be able to register
the fake County Court Judgment onto our credit file to
cause us damage.

These so-called orders are in fact prima facie evidence
of a fraud and can be used as evidence against them in
our claim.

Chapter Ten

Tort

Tort law in the United Kingdom is an essential aspect of civil law, governing the rights and obligations of individuals and entities in relation to civil wrongs.

Its origins can be traced back to ancient legal systems, such as the Roman law concept of delict, a term in civil and mixed law jurisdictions whose exact meaning varies from jurisdiction to jurisdiction but is always centered on the notion of wrongful conduct.

In medieval England, the notion of torts began to take shape, primarily as a means of resolving disputes outside the criminal justice system. Initially torts were categorised as either trespass or trespass on the case, with the former involving direct physical harm and the latter covering indirect or consequential harm.

The development of tort law in England was heavily

influenced by the common law system, relying on judicial decisions and precedents. Throughout the centuries, judges gradually shaped the principles and doctrines that form the foundation of modern tort law.

A significant milestone in its evolution was the case of Ashby v White (1703) in which the case established the principle that an individual who suffers a legal injury has the right to seek compensation, regardless of whether the injury caused any physical harm. This expanded the scope to encompass not only direct physical harm but also intangible harms, such as interference with rights.

Another crucial development occurred with the landmark case of Donoghue v Stevenson (1932), which established the modern concept of duty of care. The case introduced the "neighbour principle," stating that individuals owe a duty of care to those who might be directly affected by their actions. It laid the groundwork for negligence claims and had a profound impact on tort law in the UK.

The common law system allowed for the flexible development of tort law, as judges had the authority to interpret and adapt the law to accommodate changes in societal circumstances. This however, also meant that the law could be subject to inconsistency and uncertainty, and prompted the need for legislative intervention and reform.

In response to the challenges posed by the common law system, the UK government enacted the Tort Reform Act of 1947 that aimed to clarify and codify certain aspects of tort law and provide a more structured framework for resolving civil wrongs. The Act codified principles related to negligence, contributory negligence, and damages, thereby bringing greater consistency to tort claims.

The Law Reform (Contributory Negligence) Act 1945 brought another significant legislative development by introducing the concept of proportionate liability. This allowed the courts to apportion responsibility for an injury between multiple parties, based on their respective degrees of negligence. This Act aimed to strike a fair balance between the principles of individual responsibility and the need for proportionate compensation.

The Law Reform (Personal Injuries) Act 1948 addressed the issue of damages in personal injury cases by establishing the principle that damages should be assessed based on the financial and non-financial losses suffered by the injured party, including pain, suffering, loss of earnings, and medical expenses. This Act provided a more structured approach to determining compensation in personal injury claims.

Negligence

Negligence is now a fundamental concept in tort law and provides a basis for many civil claims. To establish a claim of negligence, the claimant is required to prove essential elements:

The Duty of Care

The defendant must owe a duty of care to the claimant. This duty arises when they should have foreseen that their actions or omissions might cause harm to others. The existence of a duty of care is determined by the courts, in considering factors such as the relationship between the parties, the foreseeability of harm, and the social and affective considerations involved.

The claimant must demonstrate that the defendant breached their duty of care. A breach occurs when the defendant fails to meet the standard of care expected of a reasonable person in similar circumstances. The standard is entirely objective, meaning that the defendant's conduct is compared to what any other reasonable person would have done.

Causation:

The claimant must establish a causal connection between the defendant's breach of duty and the harm suffered. There are two components of causation and the claimant must establish both factual causation and legal causation.

Factual causation, also known as the "but-for" test, requires a demonstration that the harm would not have occurred "but for" the defendant's breach of duty.

Legal causation, on the other hand, involves determining whether the defendant's breach was a significant and direct cause of the harm suffered.

Remoteness of Damage

Remoteness of damage refers to the principle that a defendant is only liable for harm that was reasonably foreseeable as a consequence of their breach of duty. The legislation sets limits on the extent to which a defendant should be held responsible for the consequences of their actions, which ensures that defendants are not held liable for unforeseeable or highly unlikely events.

The test for remoteness of damage is often referred to as the "reasonable foreseeability" test and asks whether a reasonable person in the defendant's position would have foreseen the type of harm that actually occurred as a result of their breach of duty. If the harm was too remote or unforeseeable, the defendant may not be held liable for it.

As the claimant, we must demonstrate that we suffered actual harm or damages as a result of the defendant's breach of duty. Damages can include physical injuries, financial losses, emotional distress, or other forms of harm recognised by legislation. The purpose of damages in negligence cases is to compensate the claimant for losses and restore them, as far as possible, to the pre-injury position.

Vicarious Liability

Vicarious liability is a legal principle that holds one party (the defendant) responsible for the wrongful acts or omissions committed by another party (the tortfeasor) who is in a legal relationship with the defendant. Under this doctrine, the defendant may be held liable for the tortious actions of another person, even if they themselves did not directly commit the wrongful act.

The rationale behind vicarious liability is based on the idea of allocating responsibility and ensuring that those who benefit from a particular relationship or enterprise also bear the burden of any harm caused by individuals acting on their behalf. This is grounded in ideas of fairness, social policy, and the recognition that certain relationships give rise to the potential for harm.

One of the most common applications of vicarious liability is in the context of employer-employee relationships. In this scenario, an employer might be held vicariously liable for the tortious actions of their employees if those actions were committed in the course of employment.

For vicarious liability to apply, the following conditions must generally be met:

1. There must be an employer-employee relationship between the defendant and the tortfeasor. This relationship can arise through a contract of employment, agency relationship, or other legal arrangements.

2. The wrongful act must have occurred within the course of the employee's employment. While the precise boundaries of the course of employment may vary depending on the circumstances, generally, an act will

be considered within the course of employment if it was authorised by the employer or closely connected to the employee's duties.

Vicarious liability has significant implications for employers as it can impose liability for the actions of their employees, even if the employer did not directly participate in or have knowledge of the wrongful act.

The doctrine serves important policy objectives, such as ensuring that victims of tortious acts are provided with a source of compensation, and encouraging employers to take reasonable steps to prevent harm caused by their employees.

Case Law and its Impact on UK Tort Legislation

As mentioned above, in the case of Donoghue v Stevenson (1932), the House of Lords established the "neighbour principle," which states that individuals owe a duty of care to those who might be directly affected by their actions.

This principle expanded the duty of care beyond immediate physical proximity and established a broader duty owed to those who, it could be reasonably foreseen would be affected by one's actions.

The duty of care is a fundamental element in tort law, particularly in negligence claims as it establishes the legal obligation of individuals to act in a manner that does not cause foreseeable harm to others. The concept has evolved over time through judicial decisions, with

141

courts refining and expanding its scope to adapt to ever-changing societal expectations and circumstances.

Caparo Industries plc v Dickman (1990)

In the subsequent years, the courts faced the challenge of defining the scope of the duty of care in specific contexts. The landmark case of Caparo Industries plc v Dickman (1990) introduced the "Caparo test" which provided a framework for determining the existence of a duty of care in negligence claims.

According to the Caparo test, three elements must be satisfied to establish a duty of care:

(i) Foreseeability of Harm
The harm suffered by the claimant must have been reasonably foreseeable by the defendant.

(ii) Proximity
There must be a relationship of proximity between the defendant and the claimant, which can be based on physical proximity, a contractual relationship, or reliance on the defendant's skill or expertise.

(iii) Fair, Just, and Reasonable
It must be fair, just, and reasonable to impose a duty of care on the defendant in the circumstances.

The Caparo test clarified the approach to determining the duty of care and provided a structured framework for the courts to assess negligence claims in various contexts.

Under Tort law we have a right of restitution based on the damage that has been caused to our commercial standing. With an impacted credit rating we find it difficult to obtain (access) our natural right to create credit and form contracts with other parties mainly due to their reliance on said credit rating. We may or may not be a bad risk, but the damage reflected in our credit file was caused through our being a conscious and fair-minded individual seeking to act according to the laws governing our actions. Punishment via negative credit file reporting for actions we undertake in highlighting bad form, deceit and outright fraudulent activity by a rogue corporation is not a legal defence for their actions towards us, or a sustainable baseline for encouraging proper behaviour in commerce.

Chapter Eleven

Data Protection

The UK Data Protection Act 2018 governs the protection and processing of personal data in the United Kingdom. Enacted in 2018, it reflects the requirement for safeguarding our privacy rights while facilitating a legitimate use of our personal information.

Every territory throughout the word has similar, or the same legislation, and much of what is contained in the UK Act can be used everywhere once corresponding versions have been located in the legislation of your territory.

The UK Act of 2018 builds upon its predecessor, the Data Protection Act 1998, and aligns itself closer to the European Union's General Data Protection Regulation (GDPR).

The revised Act enhanced data protection standards, promoted transparency, strengthened individual rights, and fostered responsible data processing practices, as well as establishing a comprehensive legal framework for regulating the collection, storage, use, and disclosure of personal data.

The DPA applies to both automated and manual processing of personal data by organisations and individuals, and defines key terms, including personal data, data subjects, data controllers, data processors, and special categories of personal data.

As well as outlining several fundamental principles that organisations must adhere to when processing personal data, such as lawfulness, fairness, transparency, purpose limitation, data minimisation, accuracy, storage limitation, integrity, confidentiality, and accountability; it also sets out the legal basis for processing personal data, such as the necessity of processing for the performance of a contract, compliance with a legal obligation, consent, protection of vital interests, the performance of a task carried out in the public interest, and legitimate interests pursued by the data controller or a third party.

Data controllers are required to provide us with transparent and concise information regarding the processing of our personal data, including the purpose, legal basis, retention period, and rights of the data subjects.

We have the right to request access to our personal data held by data controllers, free of charge and the Act sets out the procedures and timelines for responding to such requests.

We also have the right to rectify inaccurate or incomplete data and request its erasure under specific circumstances, such as when the data is no longer necessary for the purpose it was collected or when consent is withdrawn.

We can deny permission for the processing of our personal data in certain situations, including direct marketing and we also have the right to restrict the processing of our data under specific circumstances.

The DPA introduces safeguards for individuals subjected to solely automated decision-making processes, including the right to human intervention, the right to express our point of view, and the right to challenge automated decisions.

Organisations may be required to appoint a DPO (data protection officer) responsible for overseeing data protection practices, advising on compliance, and acting as a point of contact for data subjects and regulatory authorities.

Organisations must demonstrate accountability by implementing appropriate data protection policies, conducting data protection impact assessments (DPIAs) for high-risk processing activities, and maintaining records of their data processing activities.

The Act allows for the free flow of personal data between the UK and other countries or territories with adequate data protection standards, as determined by the UK government.

It also provides provisions for data transfers outside the UK, including standard contractual clauses, binding corporate rules, and adequacy decisions by the UK Information Commissioner's Office (ICO).

The DPA emphasises cooperation and mutual assistance between the ICO and supervisory authorities in other countries, promoting consistent data protection enforcement and the exchange of information.

The ICO is the primary regulatory body responsible for enforcing the UK Data Protection Act. It has the power to investigate breaches, issue warnings and reprimands, impose administrative fines, and conduct audits and inspections. Just the fact that the ICO exists is a telling situation about the state of play with the morality of business these days.

The DPA introduces substantial penalties for non-compliance, including administrative fines of up to a certain percentage of an organisation's global annual turnover or a fixed amount, depending on the severity of the infringement and size of business engaged in the breach.

Those who have suffered damage as a result of a breach of the Act have the right to seek compensation from the data controller or processor responsible. They may also seek remedies through judicial proceedings.

Organisations must ensure compliance with the UK Data Protection Act by implementing appropriate technical and organisational measures, conducting privacy impact assessments, and maintaining comprehensive documentation of data processing activities.

The Act mandates organisations to report certain types of personal data breaches to the ICO within a specified timeframe. Those affected by a breach that poses a high risk to their rights and freedoms must also be notified.

Organisations engaging in international data transfers must assess the adequacy of data protection standards in the recipient country, implement appropriate safeguards, and establish data transfer mechanisms to ensure lawful and secure data flows.

The Act promotes the integration of data protection measures from the outset of any data processing activity. Privacy considerations, like data minimisation and security, must be built into systems, processes, and products by design and by default.

The Data Protection Act 2018 provides us with clear and actionable remedy without too much fuss. That the ICO is a very active entity is self-evident with cases making the news on a weekly basis.

Regarding the particular onion that we're about to peel, the truth of the matter has been staring us in the face since the beginning of our dealings with the bank and provides an excellent basis for claim under DPA breach.

To state that position simply: the bank *never* had a legal position with regards to our personal data.

The total failure of the contract from the outset means that no legal relationship exists between the parties, thus, they have no rights to our private information that can be supported by any legal mechanism. That they collected it, retained and used it, and then shared it with third parties (DCA's and credit file agencies) immediately qualifies as a full breach of the entire Act.

(More about this later)

Chapter Twelve

Restitution

Restitution is a legal concept aimed at restoring the claimant to their original position by requiring the wrongdoer to return or compensate for their ill-gotten gains. It's a remedy based in the principle of unjust enrichment, ensuring that one party does not unjustly benefit at the expense of another.

Restitution operates on three core principles:

1. unjust enrichment

2. absence of a valid legal basis

3. the requirement of a causal connection

Where unjust enrichment refers to the idea that a person should not be allowed to benefit at the expense of another in situations where it would be inequitable to do so, restitution focuses on restoring the status quo by removing any enrichment that lacks a valid legal basis.

To establish a claim in restitution, the claimant must demonstrate that the enrichment is unjust and arises from a lack of legal justification.

Restitution requires the presence of certain elements.

1. There must be a benefit conferred upon the defendant by the claimant.

2. The claimant must have suffered a corresponding detriment or loss.

3. There must be a connection between the benefit and the detriment, establishing a causal link.

4. The enrichment must be unjust, meaning that the defendant has obtained a benefit at the claimant's expense without a legal basis.

5. There should be no defences available to the defendant that would bar the claimant's right to restitution, such as change of position or bona fide purchaser defences.

Restitution offers various remedies to address unjust enrichment, with the two primary remedies being restitutionary damages and restitutionary disgorgement.

Restitutionary damages aims to compensate the claimant for the loss suffered as a result of the defendant's unjust enrichment. It seeks to put the claimant into the position they would have been, if the unjust enrichment had not occurred.

Restitutionary disgorgement on the other hand, focuses on stripping the defendant of their unjust gains and returning them to the claimant. It aims to prevent the defendant from retaining any benefit acquired through unjust means.

While the principles and remedies of restitution are well established, certain considerations can complicate its application and these include the tracing of funds (finding where the money went), the role of change of position defences, the availability of proprietary remedies, and the interaction of restitution with other areas of law, such as contract and tort.

Tracing funds is crucial in establishing a connection between the benefit and detriment, especially in complex financial transactions. Change of position defences may arise when the defendant has innocently changed their position in reliance on the benefit received. Proprietary remedies can be available when the claimant seeks to assert a proprietary interest in the defendant's property.

Lastly, the interplay between restitution and other areas of law requires careful analysis to ensure coherence and avoid conflicting outcomes.

Subrogation

"Subrogation ...is a remedy, not a cause of action. It is available in a wide variety of different factual situations in which it is required in order to reverse the defendant's unjust enrichment. Equity lawyers speak of a right of subrogation, or an equity of subrogation, but this merely reflects the fact that it is not a remedy which the court has a general discretion to impose whenever it think it just to do so.

The equity arises from the conduct of the parties on well-settled principles and in defined circumstances that make it unconscionable for the defendant to deny the proprietary interest claimed by the plaintiff. A constructive trust arises in the same way.

Once the equity is established the court satisfies it by declaring that the property in question is subject to a charge by way of subrogation in the one case or a constructive trust in the other."

Millet L. J. in *Boscawen v Bajwa*.

The following excerpts are taken from the legal tome "The Law of Restitution" Seventh Edition by Lord Goff of Chiveley, PC, DCI, FBA, and Gareth Jones, Q,C., LL.D., F.B.A. Published by Sweet & Maxwell 2007.

ISBN 13 978 0421 926004

(3-006)
The role of subrogation in the law of restitution

The equity arises from the conduct of the parties. Consequently it is not true to say that it does "not arise until the court made the necessary order. The order merely [satisfies] a pre-existing equity." In order to satisfy that "pre-existing equity" a claimant must demonstrate that the defendant has been unjustly enriched at his expense.

Because of the tripartite relationship of the parties, it is not always easy to determine whether it is B or C who has been enriched and why a court should conclude that the enrichment is an unjust enrichment, although it may be clearer that the enrichment is at A's expense."

(3-009)
When is it just to allow subrogation?

An examination of the decided case law demonstrates that subrogation may be deemed to be an appropriate remedy for a number of different reasons. A may have paid under a mistake of fact, under compulsion; for a consideration which totally failed; to protect his interest in property of which he was the co-owner; or B's conduct may be said to have been unconscionable. As Buckley L.J. once said:

"The relevant equitable considerations may depend on the nature of the case. They may be different, for example where the basis of subrogation is a contract of indemnity, or where the problem is associated with *ultra vires* borrowings by a company; or where ... a lender lends money which is used for completing a purchase or for paying off an existing mortgage."

(3-025)
The basis of subrogation

A surety who pays off the debt owed by the principal debtor is subrogated to any sureties given by the debtor to the creditor as security for the debt. The surety's right to have those securities transferred to him, and his right to seek contribution from a co-surety are said to be based on "a principle of natural justice." In *Craythorne v Swinburne*, Sir Samuel Romilly described why equity intervened in the following words, which gained the approval of Lord Eldon. He said:

"…a surety will be entitled to every remedy, which the creditor has against the principal debtor; to enforce every security and all means of payment; to stand in the place of the creditor; not only through the medium of contract, but even by means of securities, entered into without the knowledge of the surety; having a right to have those securities transferred to him; though there was no stipulation for that; and to avail himself of all those securities against the debtor. This right of a surety also stands not upon contract, but upon a principle of natural justice: the same principle upon which one surety is entitled to contribution from another."

Subrogation is not then based on contract, for the surety "seldom if ever stipulated for the benefit of the security which the principal debtor has given." Its basis is natural justice. It is against conscience for the debtor to regain the securities from the creditor on the discharge of the debt by the surety, because it is the debtors obligation to indemnify the surety against any loss he incurs.

(3-026)
The extent of subrogation

The surety's right does not depend on his knowledge of the existence of any security: and after some doubt, as security for the debt must be handed to the surety who pays off the debt, even though they were additional securities given after the contract of guarantee was made, even though they only came into existence after the making of the contract guarantee, and even though they are deemed to be satisfied by the payment of the debt.

Mortgage securities held by the mortgagee creditor are not *Sui generis* and must be transferred to the surety on payment of the debt.

(24-006)
When will a restitutionary claim be successful?

It is clear that where a statute which renders a transaction illegal expressly grants a right of recovery to the claimant, he will, of course, be entitled to recover his money in spite of the illegality. Thus, a premium paid by a tenant to a landlord, contrary to the provisions of the Rent Restrictions Act, may be recovered by the tenant. But the mere fact that a transaction is rendered illegal under a statute which protects persons in the position of the claimants does not mean that they have an equitable proprietary claim.

In *Box and others v Barclaycard* the claimants deposited money with a company which ran an unauthorised deposit money business, contrary to the Banking Act 1987, s3. The company deposited the money in an account, which was overdrawn at all material times, with the defendant bank. Ferris J. rejected the submission that, since the contracts of deposits were affected by illegality, equity would impose a constructive trust to enable the plaintiffs to recover the money. Section 3(3), which states that the "fact that a deposit has been taken in contravention of this section shall not affect any civil liability arising in respect of the deposit or the money deposited", "leaves the ordinary contractual remedies of the depositor intact." It is true that section 3 was intended to protect depositors in the position of the claimants. But they would be afforded that protection by the recognition of their personal claims under the contracts of deposit. If the contracts had been valid, their claims would be personal. It would be absurd to put them in a better position because of the illegality, thereby preferring them to other general creditors.

(24-013)
Where the parties are not in *pari delicto (equally at fault)*

Where the claimant has paid money to the defendant under an illegal contract, the illegality is unknown to the claimant because of some mistake of fact, he is entitled to recover his money in an action for money had and received, if he has not got what he bargained for. Thus, in *Oom v Bruce,* the plaintiff as agent for a Russian subject abroad, purported to insure with the defendant goods on board the ship *ElbeI,* at and from St Petersburg to London, and paid a premium under the policy. Unknown to the plaintiff, Russia had commenced hostilities against Great Britain shortly before the insurance was effected, and the policy was therefore illegal. The Court of King's Bench held that the plaintiff was entitled to recover the premium. The plaintiff's mistake was one of fact. Today his restitutionary claim will succeed even if the mistake was one of law.

Where parties enter into a contract which can be

performed in a legal manner, which the defendant without the claimant's knowledge elects to perform illegally, it has been said that the defendant cannot plead its illegality. But, on discovering the illegal performance, the claimant is bound to bring the contract to an end in which event he can recover on a *quantum meruit* the value of services rendered in the performance of his side of the bargain.

So, in *Clay v Yates*, the plaintiff, a printer, agreed to print 500 copies of the defendant's treatise, to which a dedication was to be attached. "He had been furnished with the treatise without the dedication. The dedication was afterwards sent, but he had no opportunity of reading it until after it was printed; he then discovered that it was libellous, and refused to permit the defendant to have it." The Court of Exchequer held that the plaintiff was justified in refusing to complete the printing of the dedication and was entitled to recover for the printing of the treatise without the dedication.

(24-014)
Fraud and pressure

There are other cases where there is "introduced the element of fraud, duress, or oppression or difference in the position of the parties which created a fiduciary relationship to the plaintiff so as to make it inequitable for the defendants to insist on the bargain that they have made with the plaintiff." In such cases, in spite of the illegality, the plaintiff is entitled to recover money paid under the transaction.

(24-015)
Fraud

In *Hughes v Liverpool Victoria Friendly Society,* the plaintiff took out five policies of insurance on lives in which she had no insurable interest. She was induced to do so by the defendant's agent, who fraudulently misrepresented that, by paying the arrears due on the premiums and keeping them up, "everything would be all right". The plaintiff later discovered that the policies were illegal and void, and brought an action against the insurance company to recover the premiums she had paid. The Court of Appeal held that, although the contract was illegal, the plaintiff was not in *pari delecto* with the defendants because she had been induced to enter into the contract by fraudulent misrepresentation.

In *Hughes'* case, the representation was one of fact. But the relief may equally be granted if the fraudulent representation was one of law. In all cases it is essential, however, that the fraud should have concealed from the plaintiff the illegal nature of the transaction.

So, in *Parkinson v College of Ambulance Ltd* and *Harrison,* the plaintiff was induced to make a large donation to a charity by the secretary's fraudulent representation that he, or the charity could and would obtain a knighthood for the plaintiff. No title was forthcoming. The plaintiff brought an action against the charity and its secretary to recover his gift as money had and received, or as damages for deceit or breach of contract. Lush J. held that he could not recover damages, as the contract was illegal and contrary to public policy; nor could he recover his money as money had and received for,

163

although there had been fraud on the part of the secretary, the plaintiff was always aware of the improper nature of the transaction. There is also jurisdiction in equity to grant relief in cases of fraud.

(32-001)
Introduction

In this section we shall consider restitutionary claims against wrongdoers. Whether such a claim succeeds may depend on the legacy of history. Equity has vigilantly protected the interests of the principals of fiduciaries, and, if they so elect, has not hesitated to compel fiduciaries not only to account for profits but to hold on trust gains made from their breach of fiduciary duty. In equity the focus of enquiry has generally been on whether there has been a breach of the fiduciary's duty of loyalty. Equity's rules were formulated in order to deliver fiduciaries from contemplating the possibility of such a breach and to strip them of any unjust enrichment.

In contrast, the primary common law remedy is damages for loss suffered. As has been seen, a restitutionary claim for the profit made from a wrongful breach of contract will succeed only in exceptional circumstances, although the confider, who consciously breaches another confidence, may be required to account for profits even though the bond of confidence arises from a contractual relationship. Whether the gain of tortfeasors must be disgorged depends, as the law now stands, on whether the title to, of possession of, the property of the injured party has been infringed. There

164

are exceptions to that general principle, the most significant of which is the tortfeasor who benefits from a criminal act.

It may be helpful to distinguish four situations.

(32-002)
The Claimant Suffers a Wrong; The Wrongdoer is Unjustly Enriched at His Expense

This class of wrongdoers includes: (i) the fiduciary who purchases trust property or a beneficial interest for his own gain, exploits trust property, or diverts an "opportunity" which otherwise would have accrued to his beneficiaries, (ii) the third party who receives trust property with the knowledge that it has been transferred in breach of trust, (iii) the confider who uses another's secret, (iv) the tortfeasor who converts the claimant's chattel, trespasses on his land or commits an act of trespass to his goods, or (possibly) passes off his goods as originating from the claimant.

(36-012)
Avoiding Statutory or Common Law bars to a Restitutionary Claim

A tortfeasor may defend himself by invoking a statutory or common law bar which appears to defeat the injured party's restitutionary claim. For example, he may point to a statutory provision or a common law rule which grants him immunity from any tortious claim. But a restitutionary claim should not necessarily fail simply because the claim in tort would fail.

The *raison d'être* of the statutory of common law bar is critical. It may then be an illegitimate extension of the policy of the statutory provision to reject the restitutionary claim for damages, which may seriously impede his social, political or economic activities. It may then be an illegitimate extension of the policy of the statutory provision to reject the restitutionary claim and allow the defendant to retain his benefit. On the other hand, that claim should fail if it would frustrate or circumvent the policy of the statute or common law rule which denies the tortious claim.

In every case the court should expressly address these questions, as did the House of Lords in the *Universe Sentinel* case. In that case the House rejected the restitutionary claim, concluding that the sections of the Trade Union and Labour Relations Act 1974 "afford an indication …of where public policy requires that line to be drawn". That conclusion is debatable; but the analysis of the questions to be answered cannot be faulted.

(38-001)
Benefits Accruing to a Criminal from his Crime

As has been seen in *Halifax Building Society v Thomas*, Thomas had obtained a 100 percent mortgage by making fraudulent misrepresentations. The building society had sold the house, paid off its mortgage, but was left with a surplus which it placed in a suspense account. However, the Crown obtained a confiscation order and sought to enforce it over Thomas' assets. The Court of Appeal held that the Crown could do so. Peter

Gibson L.J. said that, in essence, the contest was between the building society and Thomas. Furthermore, the Lord Justice continued, although the money was the direct product of Thomas' deceit, the investment was not. So, the result of the Court of Appeal's decision was that *this* criminal, Thomas, was allowed to retain the fruits of his crime.

We have already given reasons for doubting the reasoning of the Court of Appeal in this case. The building society has two distinct claims against Thomas: one as a secured creditor for its debt, and a restitutionary claim, based on Thomas' deceit, for the benefits gained from the tortious act. It can pursue both claims to judgment; if one claim has been satisfied, it must bring the sum recovered into account. Thomas was not only a tortfeasor, he was a criminal, who should not have been allowed to retain the benefits of his crime.

This chapter at first read, may seem counter productive to the outcome we seek, but in most cases highlighted, there was the inference of a bona fide contract being in place between the parties at the outset, directing performance of the parties, that was subsequently breached. Where there was no contract there was the inference of natural justice as the baseline.

The surety aspect which in our case would be a DCA (Debt Collection Agency) were (theoretically) given the right to pursue the defendant as if they were the claimant themselves.

In our situation, from the outset the bank failed at every point to launch a legally binding *legitimate* contract. That much is self-evident by their multiple failures and subsequent *lack* of enthusiasm to have the agreement looked over and enforced by a court.

So the bank has no rights or legal authority to enforce a non-existent contract - as confessed and accepted via our Affidavit process to them from the first book (The Title is Unimportant).

The question that must be asked is 'how does a DCA gain any legal right to collect on the debt (as surety, after buying the bad debt from the bank) when the originator had none?

The answer is as obvious as it is true - they don't. There is no mechanism built into the selling and buying of a bad debt that can magically and suddenly transform a non-contract into a viable contract and endow it with legitimacy. That is, and will remain to be their Achilles Heel regarding the transference of alleged 'right to collect'.

Chapter Thirteen

A Treatise on the Law of Contracts

Joseph Chitty (1776–1841) was a prominent English legal scholar and barrister whose work significantly impacted the legal landscape.

He was revered for his profound understanding of law and extensive legal writings, and Chitty remains an influential figure in the history of English jurisprudence.

Born in London in 1776, Chitty was the son of a bookseller and began his education at a young age. He displayed an outstanding intellect, particularly in legal studies. He entered the legal profession and was called to the Bar at the Middle Temple in 1804, where he quickly gained recognition for his legal acumen and expertise.

Chitty's legal career spanned several decades, during which he made substantial contributions to the field through his writings and professional practice. He excelled in various areas of law, particularly in the realms of commercial law, criminal law, and practice, leaving a permanent mark on each.

One of Chitty's most enduring legacies lies in his extensive work as an author where his publications are regarded as authoritative texts and remain highly regarded in legal circles. Notably, his contributions to the field of law include "A Practical Treatise on Bills of Exchange" and "A Treatise on the Law of Contracts."

These works provided comprehensive insights into their respective subjects and became essential references for legal practitioners and scholars.

Chitty's meticulous research, coupled with his clear and concise writing style made his works accessible and invaluable to both legal professionals and students and his works celebrated for their depth of analysis. They remain widely referenced and studied to this day.

Aside from his legal writings, Chitty also distinguished himself in his professional practice as a barrister where his reputation for legal expertise and integrity earned widespread respect among his contemporaries. His advocacy skills in court were highly regarded, and he became known for his ability to present complex legal arguments persuasively.

'A Treatise on Contracts', or a version of it, is used in pretty much every courtroom and is on most lawyer's bookshelves. The work explores the fundamental principles of contract law, providing comprehensive insights into the formation, interpretation, and enforcement of contracts.

The treatise is divided into several sections, each addressing the different aspects of contract law. It begins by describing the nature and definition of a contract, with emphasis on the importance of mutual agreement, consideration, and intention to create legal relations. He explores the various forms of contracts, including express, implied, and quasi-contracts, and delves into the legal requirements for their validity.

One of the key contributions lies in exploration of the elements necessary for the formation of a contract. Chitty discusses the offer and acceptance, highlighting their essential characteristics and the principles governing their validity. He explains how an offer must be sufficiently definite and communicated to the offeree, who, in turn, must accept the offer unequivocally.

The treatise also explores the concept of consideration, a fundamental requirement for a contract's enforceability. He examines what constitutes valid consideration while placing great importance on the need for both parties to provide something of value in exchange. He further explores exceptions to the consideration rule, such as contracts under seal and contracts based on promissory estoppel.

He then discusses the interpretation of contracts, throwing light on the principles and rules used by courts to ascertain the parties' intentions. He explores the role of express and implied terms, as well as the significance of surrounding circumstances and trade usages in contract interpretation. Chitty's analysis provides invaluable guidance for Judges and practitioners grappling with the complexities of contractual language.

Another important aspect covered is the *capacity* of parties to enter into contracts - the legal competence required, addressing issues such as minority, mental incapacity, and undue influence.

He explains how contracts with parties lacking the necessary capacity may be voidable or void, depending on the circumstances.

The treatise delves into vitiating factors that can render a contract unenforceable, such as mistake, misrepresentation, duress, and illegality. He explains the different types of mistakes and their consequences, explores the impact of fraudulent, innocent, and negligent misrepresentations, and discusses the circumstances under which a contract may be considered void due to illegality.

The work also covers performance, breach, and discharge of contracts. It examines the various ways in which contractual obligations can be discharged, including through performance, agreement, frustration, and breach. He covers the concept of anticipatory breach, where one party indicates their intention not to fulfill their contractual obligations before the agreed-upon time. Chitty also discusses remedies available to the injured party in case of breach, such as damages, specific performance, injunctions, and restitution.

The book dedicates significant attention to the rules governing the assignment and delegation of contractual rights and duties, and explains the distinction between assignments and novations, highlighting the conditions necessary for a valid assignment and the potential consequences for the parties involved.

Throughout the treatise, Chitty draws upon a rich array of case law and statutes to support his analysis and provide practical examples. His meticulous examination of legal principles and authorities enhances the treatise's credibility and usefulness as a reference work.

'A Treatise on Contract' has endured the test of time due to its clarity, thoroughness, and comprehensive coverage of contract law principles. It serves as an indispensable resource for understanding the intricacies of contract formation, interpretation, performance, and remedies.

The treatise continues to be cited by courts, legal professionals, and academics worldwide, making it very influential in the field of contract law.

The following are extracts taken from the 32nd Edition for illustration. If ever there's a court scenario or tête-à-tête with a legal person over issues pertaining to contract, the following references from the book are invaluable. It will stand them up immediately and comprehensively demonstrate that you cannot, and will not be lead down the garden path during their attempts at bamboozling you with legal jargon, precisely because you understand exactly what's possible under law, and because you're citing work that they absolutely already know to be the authority on the matter.

"Chitty on Contracts Volume 2 Specific Contracts"
ISBN 0 421 691 905 Sweet & Maxwell.

(29-031)
Misrepresentation

A claim to rescind a contract for misrepresentation will normally accrue when the representee enters into the contract in reliance on the misrepresentation. Where the representee claims damages under section 2(1) of the Misrepresentation Act 1967, his cause of action will accrue when he 'suffers loss' as a result of entering into the contract. In some cases, at least, he will suffer loss when the transaction into which he has been induced to enter is implemented. In other cases, however, he will not suffer loss until even later, when he incurs expenditure or sustains other damage in consequence of

176

entering into the contract.

(30-001)
Common Law

Lord Wright has described the nature of restitution or quasi-contract in *Fibrosa Spolka Akcyjna v Fairbairn Lawson Combe Barbour Ltd [1943] A.C. 32,61.*

"It is clear that any civilised system of law is bound to provide remedies for cases of what has been called unjust enrichment or unjust benefit, that is, to prevent a man from retaining the money of, or some benefit derived from, another which it is against conscience that he should keep. Such remedies in English law are generically different from remedies in contract or in tort, and are now recognised to fall within a third category of the common law which has been called quasi-contract or restitution."

(30-003)
Equity

The common law has not been alone in providing a remedy for unjustifiable enrichment. Equity independently developed some principles which are aimed at the same result, *viz.* to force a man to disgorge property in his possession which rightly "belongs" to the claimant. In equity, restitutionary principles have been influential in a number of ways; first in the "constructive" trust, whereby a man was deemed to be a trustee of the property for the claimant, so that many

of the remedies of the law of trusts were available to enable the claimant as beneficiary to recover what was due to him."
Secondly, there is the mechanism of the tracing order, whereby property in the wrong hands could be "followed" or "traced" by the true owner despite changes in or admixture of the property.

Thirdly, the doctrine of acquiescence has enabled relief to be given to a person who has expended money on the property of another. In the United States these different principles of common law and equity have been amalgamated into a single topic in the law called "Restitution," as is evidence by the volume published in 1937 entitled *The American Law Institute's Restatement of the Law of Restitution, Quasi-Contracts and Constructive Trusts.* English lawyers are now aware of the interrelation of law and equity in the field of quasi-contract and restitution, and it has no need to treat the action for money had and received and an action for an equitable remedy "as any longer depending upon different concepts of justice." Accordingly in this chapter some indication will be given of the scope of equitable remedies.

(30-009)
The principle of unjust enrichment

The American Law Institute's *Restatement of the Law of Restitution, Quasi-Contracts and Constructive Trusts* concisely states that "a person who has been unjustly enriched at the expense of another is required to make restitution to the other." Although there is no general cause of action in English law for unjust enrichment, it has recently been explicitly recognised by the House of Lords in *Lipkin Gorman v Karpnale Ltd* that the concept of unjust enrichment lies at the heart of and is the principle underlying the individual instances in which the law does give a right to recovery. However, despite the strong support of several judges including Lords Wright, Atkin, Denning, Pearce and Goff and numerous academic writers, the precise shape of English law has until recently been formed against a background of skepticism.

In 1760 Lord Mansfield sought to rationalize the action for money had and received to the use of the claimant in the following well-known passage:

"This kind of equitable action to recover back money which ought not in justice to be kept is very beneficial, and therefore much encouraged. It lies for money which, *ex aequo et bono*, the defendant ought to refund; it does not lie for money paid by the plaintiff, which is claimed of him as payable in point of honour and honesty, although it could not have been recovered from him by any course of law; as in payment of a debt barred by Statute of Limitations, or contracted during his minority, or to the extent of principal and legal interest upon a serious contract, or for money fairly lost at play: because in all of these cases the defendant may retain it with a safe conscience, though by positive law he was debarred from recovering. . . . [T]he gist of this kind of action is that the defendant, upon the circumstances of the case, is obliged by the ties of natural justice and equity to refund the money."

(30-011)

The criticism that the principle of unjust enrichment is too vague to be of any practical use overlooks the fact that there is already a considerable body of case law dealing with the categories of restitution, so that judges are not called upon to use their own sense of justice in order to apply or develop the law. The judges will follow the existing precedents, which cover most of the likely problems of restitution, and if an extension of the law is sought, the meaning to be attached to "unjust enrichment" will be gleaned from the precedents. Lord Mansfield's view of quasi-contractual obligation was accepted by many in the nineteenth century, though it has been attacked in the first half of this century by judicial and academic adherents of the "implied contract" theory. However, in recent years Lord Mansfield's approach has been strongly supported and was relied on in the decisions of the House of Lords developing the law by recognizing the defence of change of position, the liability to make restitution of *ultra vires* receipts of tax, and of money paid in pursuance of an ineffective contract.

(30-012)

The principle has also been recognised by statute. The Torts (Interference with Goods Act 1977,s.7(4) imposes a liability to reimburse upon a person who, as a result of enforcement of a double liability in proceedings for wrongful interference with goods, is "unjustly enriched to any extent." Furthermore, the separation in the

Insolvency Act 1986, s.382(4), of liabilities arising out of contract, tort, trust and bailment from those "arising out of an obligation to make restitution" may provide implicit support for the principle of unjust enrichment and the statutory power to refund overpayments of rates has been said to create "a statutory remedy of restitution . . . to prevent the unjust enrichment of the rating authority at the expense of the ratepayer." Finally, statutory rights to recover overpaid tax are subject to the *defence* that repayment would unjustly enrich the claimant.

(30-013)

In conclusion, it does not follow from the absence of a general cause of action in English law for unjust enrichment that the specific remedies provided are not justifiable by reference to the principle of unjust enrichment even if they were originally framed without primary reference to it and the modern cases show an increasing tendency to cut through technicality to perceive and define the underlying principle. The historical development of the subject has affected the way the principle manifests itself: thus English law has not recognised a general action for the recovery of money on the ground that it was not due, a *conditio indebiti,* but as we shall see, has recognised specific grounds which a plaintiff seeking restitution must establish. English law has now joined United States jurisdictions, Australian law, Canadian law, Scots law, French law and Roman-Dutch law in accepting the principle of unjust enrichment. It is now widely regarded as the correct theoretical principle of

181

restitution since the alternative theory, now to be considered, is obviously inadequate. Where one is concerned with a restitutionary remedy, the appropriate questions are therefore, "first, whether the defendant would be enriched at the claimant's expense; secondly, whether such enrichment would be unjust and thirdly, whether there are nevertheless reasons of policy for denying a remedy. Notwithstanding the acceptance of unjust enrichment as the basis of most restitutionary obligations, as is submitted elsewhere in this chapter, in a number of situations it is preferable to see the basis of liability as the protection of the claimant's reasonable reliance.

(30-015)

"It would indeed be a *reductio ad absurdum* of the doctrine of precedents. In fact, the common law still employs the action for money had and received as a practical and useful, if not complete or ideally perfect, instrument to prevent unjust enrichment, aided by the various methods of technical equity which are also available, as they were found to be in *Sinclair v Brougham.*

The principle of unjust enrichment requires first, that the defendant has been "enriched" by the receipt of a "benefit", secondly, that this enrichment is "at the expense of the claimant," and thirdly that the retention of the enrichment be "unjust". The development of the law of restitution in England has meant that the principle of unjust enrichment has not manifested itself in a general action for the recovery of money paid and
182

other benefits conferred on the ground that they were not due but as a number of specific substantive grounds upon which restitution may be ordered.

In *Moses v Macferlen*, Lord Mansfield stated that the action for money had, and received, "lies for money paid by mistake: or upon a consideration which happens to fail; or for money got through imposition (express or implied); or extortion; or an undue advantage taken of the claimant's situation, contrary to the laws made for the protection of persons under those circumstances. Where a sum has been paid which is not due but the payer cannot establish a ground for recovery, it is not recoverable. But the non-recognition of the principle of unjust enrichment in the past has meant that the concepts of "benefit", "at the expense of the claimant" and "unjustness" of retention have tended to develop in a fragmented way within the substantive categories in which relief has been given and sometime, as in the former rules that only mistakes as to liability gave rise to restitution and that in general a payment under a mistake of law was not recoverable, in an unsatisfactory way.

(30-017)

Where a ground upon restitution may be granted is established, relief will nevertheless not be granted if it would not be "unjust" to allow the defendant to retain that received at the claimant's expense. Restitution is denied where the defendant cannot be restored to his original position, is a bona fide purchaser, or where the public policy precludes restitution, or the plaintiff is estopped.

It is also denied where the benefit was conferred:

a) As a valid gift

b) pursuant to a valid common law, equitable or statutory obligation owed by the claimant to the defendant

c) by the claimant while performing an obligation owed to a third party

d) by the claimant acting voluntarily in his own self-interest

e) in submission to an honest claim, under process of law or a compromise of a disputed claim and;

f) by the claimant acting "voluntarily" or "officiously"

Although some statutes do not explicitly envisage restitutionary claims as a third category, others do. Thus the definition of liability in the Insolvency Act 1986, s.382(4), includes liabilities "arising out of an obligation to make restitution" as well as those arising for breach of trust or contract, or in tort and bailment and the Torts (Interference with Goods) Act 1977, s.7(4) imposes liability on a person who is "unjustly enriched".

The underlying of the precedents seems to be an obligation upon the defendant to make restitution of a benefit which he ought not in justice to retain at the expense of the claimant. A restitutionary or quasi-contractual situation resembles a contractual one in that liability is imposed upon a particular person to pay money to another particular person, yet it differs radically in that restitutionary liability is imposed by the law irrespective of the agreement of the parties.

English lawyers are now aware of the interrelation of law and equity in the field of quasi-contract and restitution with Equity law independently developing some principles that are aimed at the same result "to force a man to disgorge property in his possession which rightly 'belongs' to the claimant".

(30-018)
The nature of the enrichment

This may take the form of a direct addition to the recipient's wealth, such as by the receipt of money, or an indirect one, for instance where an inevitable expense has been saved. The most common example of the second type of benefit is the discharge of an obligation of the defendant, whether by paying his creditor or abating a nuisance or performing some other service for which he is primarily responsible.

(30-026)
Mistake of fact: "Supposed liability" rule

It has long been clear that money paid under a mistake of the payer as to a material fact is, in certain circumstances recoverable. Mistake in this context means lack of knowledge but it is notoriously difficult to make an authoritative statement of the principles upon which recovery is based. Broadly speaking, there are two approaches; one based on the nature of the mistake permitting recovery only for certain types of mistake, the other, which now prevails, based on the effect of the mistake, prima facie permitting recovery whenever the mistake causes the payment.

Much of the difficulty seems to be due to the application of dicta, made in the context of particular facts, to quite different facts, as if the established principles of general application. Thus, while the decision of the court of Exchequer in *Kelly v. Solari* can be seen as the basis of the modern law, the statements of Parke B. can lead to distortion if accepted as a definition of the boundaries of recovery. He said that "where money is paid to another under the influence of a mistake, that is upon the supposition that a specific fact is true, which would entitle the other to the money, but which fact is untrue, and the money would have not been paid if it had been known to the payer that the fact was untrue, an action will lie to recover it back".

In *Sybron Corporation v. Rochem Ltd* a payment of accrued benefits under a pension scheme which provided that in cases of early retirement such benefits were to be dealt with at the discretion of the trustees, was made in ignorance of the payee's breach of duty to disclose the fraud of his subordinates with whom he acted. The accrued benefits had been paid under a mistake of fact induced by the payee's breach of duty and the Curt of Appeal allowed the payer to recover.

(30-030)
Fundamental Mistake

It has been said that recovery of mistaken payments can legitimately be granted on a generous basis where there is no contract that would need to be avoided because the policy favouring finality of contract does not apply if there is no transaction to rescind except the payment itself.

Furthermore, the word "mistake" in this context not only signifies a positive belief in the existence of something which in reality does not exist, but it may also include forgetfulness and sheer ignorance of something relevant to the transaction.

It is possible that the requirement that the mistake be fundamental in fact involves no more than that, without the mistake, the payment would not have been made. A payment made by an agent acting under a mistake of fact is recoverable although the principal himself, or another agent, knows the true facts. If however the payment is due under a contract between the payer and the payee, the payment cannot be recovered unless the contract itself is held void or is discharged.

(30-031)
Can one recover wherever the mistake causes the payment?

The recognition of the principle of unjust enrichment puts into question tests based on the nature of the mistake. In *Barclays Bank Ltd v. W.J. Simms, Son and Cooke (Southern) Ltd* it was stated that "if a person pays money to another under a mistake of fact which causes him to make the payment, he is *prima facie* entitled to recover it".

Support for this causation test, which has since been recognised by the High Court of Australia, is found in speeches in several decisions of the House of Lords, most recently in *Kleinwort Benson Its v. Lincoln C.C* where it was stated that the payer "must prove that he would not have made the payment had he known of his mistake at the time when it was made" and that the function of mistake is to show that the benefit which has been received was an unintended benefit.

(30-032)
Burden of Proof

It appears that the burden of proof will not be heavy, at any rate if the mistake is serious, and it has been said that it is an "irresistible inference" that a payer who is mistaken about or ignorant of, a material fact, would not have made the payment had he known the true position, Where, however, the payer would not have appreciated the materiality of a fact recovery may be refused on the ground that the payment was made in settlement of a claim. The mistake must be the effective cause of the payment. The position is similar where the payer is aware that there is an issue of law which is relevant but, being in doubt as to what the law is, pays without waiting to resolve that doubt. A person who pays when in doubt takes the risk that he may be wrong.

(30-034)
Negligence: Payer with means of knowledge

The fact that the person paying money was in a position to discover all the relevant circumstances concerning the payment, may possibly, as a matter of evidence, support the inference that he had actual knowledge of those circumstances or that he has represented that reasonable care was used in making and checking the payment.

There is, however, no conclusive rule of law that, because a person has the means of knowledge, he must be taken to have actual knowledge. Thus, a person paying money under a mistake of fact is not prevented from recovering it merely because he was negligent in failing to discover the true facts.

Parke B. in *Kelly v. Solari,* said that recovery was possible"...however careless the party paying may have been in omitting to use due diligence to inquire into the fact". So the action for money paid under a mistake of fact lies to recover money paid to the defendant by the claimant under bona fide forgetfulness of facts which disentitle the defendant to receive it, or money paid in ignorance of a fact which the claimant could have discovered at the time of payment if he had availed himself of his means of knowledge.

(30-042)
Mistake of Law: Principles Governing Recovery

It was held that the questions raised in a claim for restitution of money paid under a mistake of law are the same as those raised in a claim for restitution of money paid under a mistake of fact: was there a mistake, did the mistake cause the payment, and did the payee have a right to receive the sum which was paid to him.

Retention of the money is prima facie unjust if the payer paid because he thought he was obligated to do so and it subsequently turns out that he was not. Lord Hope stated that although it may be more difficult to establish that there has been a mistake of law, there is no essential difference in principle with regard to the payer's state of mind or with regard to the state of facts or the law, which must be determined at the time of payment.

But his Lordship considered that there was no reason in principle for the mistake to be one that is capable of being discovered at the same time as the time when the payment was made. The prima facie right to recover a mistaken payment is subject to the ordinary defences to restitutionary claims which are concerned to protect the stability of closed transactions; *i.e.* change of position, compromise, and settlement of an honest claim, the last of which may assume an increased importance despite

190

its current somewhat uncertain scope, since many of the cases in which recovery was barred by the mistake of law rule that judgment is afterwards overruled by a higher court in a different case.

(30-048)
General Principles

Where money has been paid under a transaction that is, or becomes ineffective, the payer may recover the money provided that the consideration for the payment has totally failed. Although the principle is not confined to contracts, most of the cases are concerned with ineffective contracts.

In the context, failure of consideration occurs where the payer has not enjoyed the benefit of any part of what he bargained for. Thus, the failure is judged from the payer's point of view and "when one is considering the law of failure of consideration and of the quasi-contractual right to recover money on that ground, it is generally speaking, not the promise which is referred to as the consideration, but the performance of the promise. The failure has to be total because the consideration is "whole and indivisible", and the courts will not divide or apportion it unless the parties have done so.

(30-062)
Benefits conferred under a void contract

Many instances of restitution on the ground of total

failure of consideration may be placed under this heading. If a contract is void *ab initio* for mistake, any payment or credit received made under the apparent contract is recoverable, and an action of wrongful interference with property may be brought in respect of goods delivered under the apparent contract.

Thus, where the claimant paid the purchase-money for an annuity on the life of A, but both parties were ignorant of the fact that A had died some days previously, he was entitled to recover the whole of the money since the contract lacked subject matter and was therefore void: the consideration had totally failed.

Again, where a company had paid instalments under a distributorship agreement which had in fact been made before its incorporation, it was entitled to recover such instalments as were paid after its incorporation; the agreement was void and the consideration for the instalments had totally failed.

Recently, recovery in these cases has been put on a wider basis. It has been held that money paid under void interest rate swap agreements can be recovered because it has been paid for "no consideration" or in the "absence of consideration", even if benefits have been received by the payer-plaintiff and the contract has been fully performed.

Where payments have been made both ways restitution is only available to a party on the basis that he gives credit for what he has received. And, if it is possible to return the parties to the original positions.

Where a contract is rendered void by statute, it is a

matter of statutory interpretation to discover whether money paid under such an apparent contract is recoverable. For example, if a wagering contract is void under the Gaming Act 1845, money paid to the winner of the wager cannot be recovered by the loser; but money advanced on a bill of sale which is void for want of form or for non-registration may be recovered, with reasonable interest, in restitution.

(30-064)
Illegal Contracts

If money is paid under a contract which is illegal, and not merely void, the general rule is that it cannot be recovered.

(30-065)
Money paid under unenforceable contract

The mere fact that one party has paid money to another under a contract which he cannot enforce against the latter because of its non-compliance with a statute requiring written evidence or on grounds of public policy, will not entitle the party who has paid the money to recover it as on a failure of consideration, for such a contract is not void, but merely unenforceable. A total failure of consideration must be proved before restitution can be claimed in these circumstances and restitution will not, in any event, be given if it would run counter to the policy of the statute in question.

(30-070)
Duress of the person and undue influence

Duress of the person or undue influence entitles a party to a contract to void it; consequently, restitution of benefits conferred under the voidable contract will be ordered by the court, following rescission by the innocent party. Even if there has been no contract, benefits conferred on the defendant as the result of duress or undue influence by him should, in principle, be recoverable from him by a claim in restitution.

The duress will usually amount to a tort and recovery will be founded on the principles governing 'waiver of tort' considered below.

(30-071)
Actual or threatened seizure or distress of the claimant's goods.

"If a person pays money, which he is not bound to pay, under the compulsion of urgent and pressing necessity or of seizure, actual or threatened, of his goods, he can recover it as money had and received. The money is not paid under duress in the strict sense of the term, as that implies duress of a person, but under the pressure of seizure or detention of goods which is analogous to that of duress."

Lord Reading C.J ~ *Maskell v. Homer [1915] 3 K.B. 106, 118*

(30-085)
Nature of obligation to make restitution

It is not entirely clear whether the restitutionary obligation is a secondary and parasitic obligation, which arises upon the violation of the primary obligation not to commit a tort, or whether the cases are instances of situations in which one set of facts gives rise to two alternative but independent causes of action, one in tort and one in restitution.

Although the authorities appear to favour the former (parasitic obligation), on the view that it is difficult to see why factors which bar the claim in tort should not also bar the claim in restitution. However, these are cases which are consistent only with the latter view. The scope of the claim in restitution depends on which is adopted. If it is the former (independent obligation) then it is a *sine qua non* of both remedies that a tort has been committed but if it is the latter then one should be available even though the other is not.

On this view, restitutionary claims in respect of benefits acquired tortiously would be an example of a broader category which includes benefits acquired by criminal acts, breach of equitable duties and, possibly, breach of statutory duties.

(30-092)
Money obtained by fraud or deceit

An important instance of this use of restitution is where the claimant uses a claim in restitution to recover money obtained from him by fraud or deceit. It has been held that, while restitution is available in respect of money paid by the claimant to the defendant, an account of profits made by the fraudulent defendant does not lie.

Thus, where the defendant obtained payment of a promissory note payable to the claimant by means of a false or forged representation of authority from the claimant, the claimant was entitled to sue the defendant in restitution to recover the money which the defendant had received. The defendant is liable to such an action even where the fraud was committed by his partner and agent, and not by him personally.

So where payments of premiums on a policy were continued by the claimant because of false representations by the defendant's agent, it was held that the premiums could be recovered by the claimant in a claim in restitution, although they might also have been recovered in an action of deceit. On the other hand, if the defendant obtains money by fraud from an agent, the agent or his principal may recover it from him.

(30-095)
Money obtained by oppression or extortion

Money obtained by illegal oppression or extortion or by taking advantage of the weak and needy may be recovered by a claim in restitution. This is another instance of a restitutionary alternative to an action in tort, since it is, in general, a tort to obtain money by unlawful intimidation.

Thus, a claim in restitution lies against a broker to recover excessive charges on a distress for rent, paid by the tenant in order to prevent a sale, even although the tenant may have applied for and obtained time in consideration of his promise to pay the charges. But where excessive charges are paid to satisfy a claim purporting to be made by virtue of a statute, but the person paying them is not oppressed or imposed on in any way, it depends on the interpretation of the particular statute whether he is entitle to recover the excess.

(30-096)
Breach of contract

A defendant may make a gain from the breach of a contract either by making a larger profit from a third party than he would have made from the other party had he performed, or by saving the expense from its breach. In general, the gain to a defendant from the breach of a contract is irrelevant to the quantification of damages. A claimant who suffers a smaller loss than the defendants gain or who suffered injury of a non-pecuniary kind from the breach of contract will find a restitutionary award attractive, and, exceptionally, the defendant's gain is relevant to the quantification of damages.

The defendant's gain is relevant in sales of land, where there has been a breach of a contractual duty of confidence or a fiduciary duty, or where the breach of contract involves the use or interference with the plaintiff's property. These are all cases of specifically enforceable contracts and it is arguable that the defendant's gains should be relevant in all such cases. It has also been suggested that, apart from specifically enforceable contracts, there are two situations in which restitutionary damages for breach of contract may be awarded where compensatory damages would be inadequate and where the defendant's profit is occasioned directly by the breach of contract and attributable to it. The first is the case of skimped performance where the defendant fails to provide the full extent of the services it contracted to provide and for which the claimant has paid.

So a gardening contractor which has agreed to attend to a garden once a week but only does so once a month might be liable to pay the sum it has saved by its breach. Secondly, a defendant who has obtained his profit by doing the very thing which he contracted not to do may be required to pay such profit to the other party.

(30-097)
Tracing orders

Where the property of the claimant can be identified to be in the hands of the defendant, the claimant as true owner of the property may "follow" or "trace" it and claim its recovery. This proprietary remedy is recognised both at common law and in equity, each with its own limitations but the equitable remedy is likely to prove more useful in practice.

The remedy is proprietary rather than personal because it may lie against an innocent recipient of the property, even where no personal claim, whether in tort, restitution, or equity, would lie against him: secondly, if the recipient of the property is insolvent, the true owner by means of a tracing order may, subject to statutory requirements in certain cases, claim specific property in priority to the claims of general creditors; thirdly, if the true owner traces his property into investments bearing interest, he will be entitled to claim the interest in addition. It has been doubted that the possibility of a claim by a third party could be a defence to a tracing claim.

(30-098)
Tracing at common law

At common law a claimant is permitted to trace and claim his property if it has not been mixed with other property but can be identified in a "physical" sense, *e.g.* sovereigns in a bag or an entire chose in action, such as a bank balance or a promissory note. If another asset has been "purchased exclusively" with the claimant's money, it is still identifiable at common law, because common law permits the owner of the original property to assert his title to the product in place of the original property and to profits made from the exchanged property. But in the case of money, identification was held not to be possible if there was "admixture of other money".

The remedy at common law may take the form of a claim for wrongful interference with goods, or an action in restitution for money had and received. The scope of the remedy in tort in particular has been considerably widened in order to protect proprietary rights; for instance, an action for conversion is given to the person on whose bank account a cheque belonging to him is drawn on his authority, the common law thus treating him as "owner" of the cheque rather than "owner" of the intangible bank balance.

These common law actions are, however, personal although the right remains proprietary and common law tracing into a substitute "cannot be relied on so as to render an innocent recipient a wrongdoer."

(30-110)
Other equitable remedies

The equitable remedy of rescission of a contract on the ground of misrepresentation or mistake may also be viewed as an instance of restitution, since the consequences of rescission include the restitution of benefits transferred by the representee in pursuance of the contract and an indemnity against liabilities necessarily incurred by the representee as a result of the contract.

Similarly, rectification of a written document which, by a mistake fails to give effect to a prior oral agreement may also lead to restitutionary relief. Likewise, equity may permit, as the result of setting aside a transaction, the recovery of benefits conferred on the defendant following undue influence exercised by the defendant over the plaintiff; it may enable restitution of benefits obtained in breach of another's confidence. Equity may also grant relief from certain unconscionable bargains.

Finally, where a person seeks to enforce a claim to an equitable interest in property, the court has a discretion to require as a condition of giving effect to that interest that an allowance be made for costs incurred and services rendered in connection with the administration of the property, The factors which will incline a court to make such an allowance include whether the work would in any event have had to be done by the person entitled to the equitable interest or a receiver appointed by the court and, the fact that the work has been of substantial benefit to the property and to the persons entitled to the equitable interest.

Chapter Fourteen

Law Reform

The Law Reform (Miscellaneous Provisions) Act 1970 was introduced to make various reforms to the law of England and Wales, particularly in relation to civil and criminal procedures. The Act was intended to streamline the legal process, reduce the burden on the courts, and make it easier for people to access justice.

Part I of the Act deals with civil procedure. It introduced several changes to the rules governing civil litigation in England and Wales and these changes included:

1. The power of the court to strike out pleadings and dismiss actions that are frivolous or vexatious.

2. The introduction of a new procedure for

summary judgment, which allows the court to dispose of a claim without a full trial if it is satisfied that there is no real prospect of success.

3. The power of the court to make interim payments to a successful party in a civil action.

4. The power of the court to make orders for security for costs, which require a party to provide security for the other party's costs in the event that the claim is unsuccessful.

Part II of the Act deals with criminal procedure. It introduced several changes to the rules governing criminal trials in England and Wales and these changes included:

1. The abolition of the rule against double jeopardy, which prevented a person from being tried twice for the same offence.

2. The power of the court to admit evidence that was obtained illegally, if it is in the interests of justice to do so.

3. The introduction of a new procedure for hearsay evidence, which allows hearsay evidence to be admitted in certain circumstances.

4. The power of the court to impose restrictions on the reporting of criminal proceedings.

Part III of the Act deals with evidence. It introduced several changes to the rules governing the admissibility of evidence in civil and criminal proceedings and these changes included:

1. The introduction of a new procedure for the admission of expert evidence, which requires experts to be independent and impartial.

2. The power of the court to order a party to produce documents or other materials for inspection.

3. The power of the court to order a party to submit to a medical examination.

Part IV of the Act deals with arbitration. It introduced several changes to the rules governing arbitration in England and Wales and these changes included:

1. The power of the court to stay legal proceedings in favour of arbitration.

2. The power of the court to order interim measures in support of arbitration proceedings.

3. The introduction of a new procedure for challenging the jurisdiction of an arbitrator.

Part V of the Act contains various miscellaneous provisions and these provisions include:

1. The power of the court to make orders for the enforcement of judgments obtained in other countries.

2. The introduction of a new procedure for the payment of damages by installments.

3. The power of the court to make orders for the payment of interest on debts and damages.

In this Act, the government clearly gave the court more discretionary powers, some that work in our favour and can be used, and some that are not quite so favourable to our cause.

Under these new 'powers' it isn't beyond the imagination to envisage a court making demands that we undergo a psychiatric / psychological evaluation to check if we're clinically insane, if say, our claims are fully against 'what everyone believes to be true' when presenting our evidence against these 'pillars of the establishment'.

It would, after all, be a masterpiece of defence if they could insist on a psychological evaluation of the claimant every time we submit our paperwork. It wouldn't take too much pressure on those 'delicate' mental health professionals to get them onside or face the potential of losing their jobs. I don't say any of this lightly, because I have seen it happen with my own eyes – twice!

Those working in the mental health sector, whilst deserving of *several* medals and salaries reflecting their particular set of skills, aren't particularly suited to the court environment and the pressures of the legal game. I've seen blatantly obvious contradictions in their statements that a child could take apart and this is primarily because the nature of their work is to dig deeply for the underlying truth of a situation and address it. When they are required to produce a certain determination that isn't quite what their tools inform them, they have a problem. One side of the claimant / defendant equation will gush over their 'findings' if it suits their agenda and discount it if not.

In any case, as a complete digression, I don't remember ever being asked whenever new Acts are introduced or that a demand by the people was submitted, so it would seem that MP's drafting proposals for bills are doing so entirely on their own behest (or being paid to do it) and are clearly doing it for the 'career advancement' opportunities it may produce, rather than as a genuine response to Public pressure to address a problem.

So we'll leave this chapter here as whilst it gives an insight of how the court views things and operates in general, there isn't all that much more to say about large corporations handing themselves even more power that inevitably works against the wishes and best interests of the people.

Chapter Fifteen

Protection from Harassment

The Protection from Harassment Act 1997 is a piece of legislation enacted in the United Kingdom to combat harassment, stalking, and other related offences. It provides for legal remedies and protections for individuals who are subjected to persistent and unwanted behaviour that causes distress, alarm, or fear.

The Act was introduced as a response to the growing recognition of the harmful effects of harassment on an individual's well being, and the need for legal measures to combat it effectively. Harassment can manifest in various forms, including unwanted communications, stalking, cyberbullying, and repeated behaviours that invade an individual's privacy or cause psychological distress.

The Act aims to provide victims with legal recourse and to deter potential offenders from engaging in such behaviour.

It defines harassment as 'a course of conduct that amounts to harassment of another individual'. Quite how something can be legally defined by using the very word that it is attempting to define is beyond me, but there it is.

The 'definition' encompasses actions that are alarming, distressing, or tormenting, and cause the victim to fear for their safety or well-being, both physical and mental.

It applies to both individuals and organisations, and recognises that harassment can occur in many different contexts, including personal relationships, workplaces, and online environments.

Under the Act, several offences are classified as criminal actions, including harassment, stalking, and putting people in fear of violence. These offences can be prosecuted in criminal courts, and individuals found guilty can face imprisonment, fines, or both.

Additionally, the Act enables victims to pursue civil remedies, such as obtaining injunctions or damages, through the civil courts. This dual approach allows victims to seek redress via criminal and civil avenues, depending on their circumstances and desired outcomes.

The Act empowers the courts to issue restraining orders and injunctions to protect victims from further harassment. Restraining orders prohibit the offender from engaging in specific behaviours, contacting the victim, or entering certain areas. Breach of a restraining order constitutes a criminal offence. Injunctions, on the other hand, can be sought by victims in civil proceedings and can provide similar protections.

The Act emphasises the importance of reporting harassment incidents promptly and ensures that victims receive appropriate support throughout the process. Victims can report incidents to the police who are then obligated under duty to investigate the allegations thoroughly. The Act also grants police officers the authority to arrest suspected offenders and take necessary measures to safeguard victims.

Victims of harassment can seek civil remedies under the Act, allowing them to take legal action against the offender. It provides victims with the opportunity to pursue compensation for the harm they have suffered, such as loss of earnings, medical expenses, and emotional distress.

The internet and social media brought new challenges in combating harassment and the Act recognises the prevalence of online harassment and enables the courts to address it reasonably effectively. Cyberbullying, online stalking, and malicious communications, provide grounds for action in empowering law enforcement agencies and courts to intervene and protect victims in the digital realm.

Despite its importance, the Act has faced criticisms and calls for reform. Some argue that penalties are not severe enough to deter potential offenders, and that improvements could be made to enhance victim protection. Also, the Act doesn't specifically address hate speech and online trolling, which are a growing concern. These concerns require further legislative action or amendments to the existing Act to ensure it remains effective and relevant in addressing evolving forms of harassment. There are other Acts that partially cover hate speech, particularly the Public Order Act 1986 but none extend into coverage of more recent incidents (and sadly – trends).

In response to these criticisms, there have been discussions regarding potential amendments to the Act to strengthen its provisions and these discussions have included proposals to increase the penalties for harassment offences, expand the definition of harassment to cover a broader range of behaviours, and specifically, address online hate speech and trolling. Personally, I think a proper legal definition of the word harassment might be a good start.

Additionally, there have been calls for improved training for law enforcement agencies and the judiciary to ensure a consistent and effective response to harassment cases.

Furthermore, the Act's enforcement and effectiveness have also been challenged due to the difficulties in gathering evidence and proving the intent of the offender, especially in online harassment cases. The anonymous nature of the internet and the global reach of online platforms pose unique challenges in investigating and prosecuting perpetrators. As technology continues to evolve, it is crucial for lawmakers and law enforcement agencies to stay abreast of new developments and adapt the legislation accordingly.

Case Law

a) Hayes v Willoughby (2013). In this case, the Court of Appeal held that for conduct to be considered harassment under the Act, it must be oppressive and unreasonable. The court emphasised that a one-off incident would not typically amount to harassment.

b) Thomas v News Group Newspapers Ltd (2001). This case involved a well-known celebrity, and the court held that the Act could be used to protect individuals from harassment by the media. It established that the Act covers not only direct contact but also indirect harassment through the publication of intrusive material.

c) Majrowski v Guy's and St. Thomas' NHS Trust (2006). This case clarified that employers can be held liable for acts of harassment committed by their employees under the Act. The House of Lords ruled that employers have a duty to prevent harassment and can be held responsible if they fail to take reasonable steps to do so.

d) Ferguson v British Gas Trading Ltd (2009). In this

case, the Court of Appeal held that a victim of harassment could bring a claim for damages under the Act, even if they did not suffer any psychiatric or psychological injury. The court recognized that harassment itself could cause distress and justified compensation.

Based on the fact that our contract with the bank never actually launched in any legal sense, and therefore is non-existent; everything they did, do, and will do regarding making demands, sending reminders, and basically, any form of contact with us, can be viewed as harassment if it causes us distress or fear.

In the case of contact by a DCA, fear, distress, and the inevitable challenges to our mental stability are always generated (as intended), as their threats of doorstep visits, telephone calls, court action, court judgments etc., are all present on the letters they send and calls they make. This isn't necessarily a bad thing for us in the long term however, as that incessant contact provides us with evidence for our case against them.

Chapter Sixteen

Administration of Justice Act 1970 Part 5

Part 5 of the Administration of Justice Act 1970 focuses on several essential aspects of the legal system in the UK. It contains provisions that touch upon the regulation of solicitors, the creation of new courts, changes to existing court structures, and other matters related to the efficient administration of justice.

One of the primary objectives of Part 5 is to enhance the regulation of solicitors. It empowers the Law Society (the regulatory body for solicitors in England and Wales) with more extensive authority to oversee the conduct and professional standards of solicitors. This increased regulatory control is vital to maintaining the integrity of the legal profession and ensuring that solicitors act in the best interests of their clients (perhaps someone should have reminded the author of the Act that a solicitor's first duty is to the court and NOT the client).

Part 5 also provides for the establishment of new courts, which was a significant development at the time. These new courts were intended to address specific needs in the judicial system. The Act granted the Lord Chancellor the authority to create these new courts and set out their jurisdictions and procedures.

In addition to the creation of new courts, Part 5 allowed for changes to existing court structures. This included adjustments to the organization and jurisdiction of the courts, reflecting evolving societal needs and legal requirements. These changes were deemed essential to ensure that the justice system remained efficient and responsive to the demands of a changing society.

Part 5 also delves into family law reform, which was a key concern at the time. The Act introduced measures to streamline and modernize family law proceedings with changes aimed at making family law cases more accessible and efficient, thereby benefiting families in times of legal need.

One of the most significant developments in Part 5 was the introduction of the tribunal system. This innovative approach aimed to address disputes and issues through specialized tribunals rather than traditional court proceedings. The tribunals were designed to provide a more accessible, cost-effective, and efficient method of dispute resolution for certain types of cases.

This change reflected a broader trend in administrative and regulatory law towards specialised decision-making bodies.

Part 5, introduced several provisions aimed at enhancing consumer protection and was particularly important in areas where individuals may be vulnerable, such as in the provision of legal services. Measures were implemented to ensure that individuals seeking legal assistance were well informed about the costs and services they could expect from their solicitors.

Part 5 of the Act also sought to improve access to justice. It recognised the importance of ensuring that individuals, **regardless of their financial means**, had access to legal representation when necessary. Provisions in this part of the Act were intended to make legal services more affordable and accessible to a wider range of people.

Judicial appointments were also addressed by establishing a formal process for selecting and appointing judges, aiming to ensure that the judiciary was composed of individuals with the necessary expertise and requisite impartiality. This process was implemented to help maintain public confidence in the legal system – and we're all waiting for it to show itself!

Legal aid, a critical aspect of ensuring access to justice for all, was another issue addressed and introduced measures to make legal aid more accessible to those who needed it most, thereby levelling the playing field in legal disputes.

The Act had a profound impact on the legal landscape in the United Kingdom for those working within it. It significantly enhanced the regulation of solicitors, introduced new court structures, and reformed family law and dispute resolution mechanisms. The creation of specialised tribunals, designed to provide more efficient and accessible justice, was a ground-breaking development and influenced the approach to dispute resolution in various areas of the law.

The Act's emphasis on consumer protection and access to justice underscored the importance of ensuring that legal services were available to all, **not just those with money**. The establishment of a formal process for judicial appointments helped maintain the independence and integrity of the judiciary.

I'd say it's high time this Act was modernised and at the very least contain the addition of liability for the man / woman acting under the protection of their indemnity / BAR registration both in front of and behind the bench.

Chapter Seventeen

The Companies Act 2006

This Act is a comprehensive piece of legislation that governs company law in the United Kingdom. It comprises over seven hundred sections and sixteen schedules, and represents a significant overhaul and modernisation of company law, replacing several older Acts.

The 2006 version covers various aspects of company formation, management, and dissolution. It introduces new provisions aimed at simplifying corporate governance, promoting shareholder rights, enhancing corporate social responsibility, and ensuring transparency.

The Act provides guidance on the procedures for establishing different types of companies, such as private and public companies limited by shares, guarantee companies, and unlimited companies. It outlines the requirements for company names, registration, and articles of association.

One of the Act's main focuses is on corporate governance where it sets out director duties, including their responsibilities to act in the company's best interests, avoid conflicts of interest, exercise reasonable care, skill, and diligence, and promote the success of the company for the benefit of its members.

Strict rules are set governing the appointment, removal, and the powers of directors by outlining their duties and responsibilities, including the duty to promote the success of the company, exercise independent judgment, and declare any conflicts of interest.

The Act strengthens shareholder rights by providing them with increased access to information, rights to propose resolutions, and the ability to challenge decisions made by the company's directors. Shareholders can also participate in decision-making processes through voting and meetings.

Also covered are the rules regarding the company's capital structure, share issuance, share buybacks, and distributions to shareholders - but none of this is particularly interesting for our purposes.

Of significant interest to our cause is where the Act imposes obligations on companies to maintain proper accounting records and prepare annual financial statements that provide a true and fair view of the company's financial position. It also sets requirements for auditing and the disclosure of financial information.

The Act provided mechanisms for the creation of regulatory bodies such as Companies House, responsible for company registration and record-keeping whilst also outlining penalties and sanctions for non-compliance, including fines, disqualification of directors, and other enforcement measures.

Since its enactment, the Companies Act 2006 has undergone various amendments and updates to adapt to evolving business landscapes and address emerging challenges. These changes aim to improve corporate governance, enhance transparency, and align with international standards.

It is the duty of all directors to exercise independent judgment, which is that directors should make decisions based on their own judgment and not be unduly influenced by external pressures or the interests of others (read shareholders and profiteering methods)

All directors are required to exercise their powers independently while making decisions in the best interests of the company; considering various factors such as the long-term success of the business, the interests of shareholders, employees, and other stakeholders, as well as safeguarding the company's reputation and impact on the community and environment, which includes the significant 'making sure the company (and themselves) don't get sued for a breach of the Act.

Directors must avoid situations where their personal interests conflict with the interests of the company and section 175 of the Act further elaborates on this duty, requiring that directors should avoid conflicts of interest and situations where they might profit personally from their position or exploit company information for personal gain.

All directors owe a fiduciary duty to the company that requires them to act honestly, in good faith, and in the best interests of the company. It includes the obligation to prioritise the company's interests above their own or any other conflicting interests.

In conjunction with exercising independent judgment, directors are expected to apply a reasonable level of care, skill, and diligence in their decision-making processes and should use their expertise and knowledge to assess situations and make informed decisions for the benefit of the company.

While directors can delegate certain tasks and responsibilities, they cannot absolve themselves of their duties. They are still ultimately accountable for the decisions made by those to whom they have delegated authority. Directors must oversee and monitor the exercise of delegated powers to ensure they align with the company's best interests.

Breach of the duty to exercise independent judgment can result in legal consequences. If directors fail to act in accordance with this duty and it results in harm to the company or it's customers, they may be held personally liable. This can involve financial penalties, legal action, and, in extreme cases, disqualification from acting as a director.

While we can extract several useable sections of the Act for our cause, my immediate attention focused on section 44 as it yields a not-so-well-hidden treasure that can be used to discredit (read entirely ignore) any and all communications from our adversaries and immediately throw the ball back to them with a charge of breach of the Act.

Section 44 is concerned with the execution of documents for ALL companies and underscores the requirement for validity. Part two of the section defines precisely what is considered to be a validly executed document and is expanded upon in detail in the subsections.

There can be no doubt about the situation as it pertains to banking and DCA practice from the perspective of their communications to us.

(2) A document is validly executed by a company if it is signed on behalf of the company —

(a) by two authorised signatories, or

(b) by a director of the company in the presence of a witness who attests the signature.

(3) The following are "authorised signatories" for the purposes of subsection (2) —

(a) every director of the company, and

(b) in the case of a private company with a secretary or a public company, the secretary (or any joint secretary) of the company.

So what does this mean for our case?

Well, in the first instance, we have seen an abundance of evidence (letters and emails etc.) from banks and DCA's where they demonstrably fail to sign off as is legally required in their communications to us. A typed signature or an illegible scrawl is commonplace on these letters and even a printing of the company name is quite common. I have never seen a director's signature let alone two, and neither have I seen a witness signature. None of this complies with the Companies Act 2006 and renders the document not just invalid but none existent.

And it's a breach of the Act.

The secondary part of the good news is that nothing they send us means anything in terms of requiring our action in the matter - legally speaking, as the Act clearly states a requirement for ALL verified documents to be signed appropriately. The fact that they aren't, literally means that they don't legally exist thus, cannot be produced in any legal action. They are produced, and often, but we only have to flag the error and poof....documents and legal point magically evaporate! Now while it could potentially be used by them as a get-out-of-jail card by claiming the letter wasn't sent by them – it still bears all the credentials and hallmarks of their company identity and of course, would then produce a full breach of the data protection Act if they claim they've been impersonated – because somehow the sender had access to all of our private information, thus their security has been compromised – still a DPA breach.

Chapter Eighteen

Citing Legislation Prior to Action

As we start unpacking the remedy offered in this work and dig into the processes involved, we need to have a look at the foundation of the method.

In the realm of law and justice, citing the appropriate legislation as a legal foundation for our case carries massive importance. It provides a solid base for our legal arguments, enhances the clarity and credibility of our claims, directs the course of the claim, and ensures adherence to legal principles. Following 'due process' ensures the best chance for our argument to succeed.

It's also very crucially where the rubber meets the road in our endeavours to bring our tormentors to account.

We can use the benefits that legislation offers, including legal certainty, persuasive power, and the promotion of a fair and just legal system (!?) to arrive at the outcome we seek.

If we want to straighten out the system and get it back on track, as it should be, we need to use it and use it properly. Hardly any case these days (certainly in my experience) correctly follows due process to the absolute letter. This is a serious fault and could, if one were reasonably proficient in the rules, be easily used to dismantle almost any case that failed to observe it properly.

One of the key advantages to citing legislation before beginning a claim is the establishment of legal certainty. Legal certainty refers to the predictability and stability of the law, which allows us to understand our rights, obligations, and available remedies.

By citing legislation to the bank / credit card company (or whomever we are dealing with) instantly provides for a clear baseline for *our* position. Our adversary's legal team are easily able to interpret where *they* stand with respect to our claim, and significantly, the protection we are offered by the legislation against their actions. This clarity reduces ambiguity and enhances the certainty of our achieving a positive outcome.

Proper citation also promotes clarity within legal arguments and by referencing specific legislation we're demonstrating that we have an understanding of the relevant provisions that we are using in our argument.

All of this combines to produce grounds that, should the courts need to be engaged at a future point, they can quickly identify the legal framework within which our dispute arises, and facilitates a more focused and effective adjudication process.

Clear and accurate citation – taken directly from the government website helps in avoiding confusion (our adversary's), and ensures that legal arguments are based in sound and well-established legal principles.

By citing the pertinent parts of the legislation - those that are applicable to our case, we gain persuasive power to the claim by grounding the arguments in the authority of legislation.

Judges and legal personnel place great weight on legal precedents and statutory provisions when making decisions, and so, by providing precise references we demonstrate our knowledge and understanding of the legal principles we are wielding. It strengthens our position and increases the likelihood of success.

Citing legislation also allows for the comparison and analysis of relevant case law. Through referencing specific statutes and Acts, we can identify similar cases to our own and the legal principles that have been established through previous judicial decisions.

We're building persuasive arguments based on legal reasoning, precedents, and legislative intent, and this can only bolster the strength of our claim.

All of this groundwork is fundamental to promoting a fair and just legal system. We're ensuring that legal principles are applied consistently and uniformly, and demonstrate equality before the law. By citing the applicable legislation, we take the work out of it for a court and enable a seamless interpretation and application of the law accurately, leading to outcomes that are predictable and consistent.

A large part of the process in this book is in our nailing down the exact part, of the exact legislation, that directly applies to our case. Our primary aim in doing this is to remove the Judge's ability to interpret the legislation and use their discretion in assessing whether the law has been correctly understood and applied. We're steering the outcome basically.

A Judge will always, wherever possible, defer to case law in any matter, because to go against the determination of his or her peers, let's say a Lord Chief Justice, would invite all manner of criticism and could potentially become a negative career move.

Lastly, our proper citation enhances public confidence in the legal system by demonstrating its adherence to established legal principles - we give the Judge an easy time of it basically. When the legislation is clear and correctly applied, it's a simple matter to reach judgment in accordance with what has gone before. And crucially, it shows everyone that the system works – which they love.

Case Law

Citing case law is an important aspect in our case as it provides foundation for legal arguments and decisions.

It plays a pivotal role in guiding the court and all parties involved, ensuring fairness, consistency, and justice.

By referencing precedent, legal professionals can quickly establish a coherent framework and evaluate the viability of the claim. It shapes legal arguments and enhances credibility.

Precedent refers to the principles and decisions set by higher courts that subsequent courts use to guide their rulings. They don't actually have to use it, but most are lazy and fall back on it - which is very handy for us. And why would they deliberately stick their neck out to go against it? (Mavericks aren't common in the legal world).

By referring to relevant cases with similar facts and legal issues, litigants and legal professionals can shape their arguments and predict potential outcomes with a reasonable degree of accuracy. Citing case law provides a basis for establishing the legal rights and obligations of parties involved.

By *our* citing of case law, we demonstrate the relevance of previously decided cases to our own argument, which encourages consistency in legal interpretation and application. It also demonstrates that we have a strong understanding of the situation and have done our homework. It sends a clear signal to all concerned that if they continue with their current path of deception then we might be tooled-up just enough to potentially take them down publicly. They will of course, already have realised all of this and will think twice before attempting any shenanigans.

The court will always seek consistency - it's crucial for maintaining public trust and confidence in the legal system, as it demonstrates that decisions are not arbitrary, but based on well-established principles.

When we cite case law we're demonstrating the depth of research and legal knowledge undertaken by us in our endeavours to get to justice. It indicates that we've thoroughly analysed prior decisions, and identified precedents that align with our own case.

By doing our due diligence we brilliantly demonstrate our ability and credibility before the court, which can significantly impact a Judge's perception of the case and the likelihood of a favourable ruling. It also removes the Judges discretion and provides them with a path to follow - which they like.

Chapter Nineteen

Process

The completion of our endeavours throughout the process (including the setup from 'The Title is Unimportant') is the production of a solid case against the bank, the DCA or anyone else that has wronged us. We'll be going at them with the full backing of legislation and common law, and as you might imagine, that leaves very little room for them to maneuver around issues and produce a defence.

Now that we've established under a legal framework, exactly what these organisations have done (and still do daily) we have to turn our attention to how we are going to apply everything we've learned to achieve our desired outcome. We must decide which of the perpetrator's infractions will gain us merit and are likely to form a strong and simple case, and which of those will be difficult or impossible to accomplish.

The approach initially is to make them an offer, and by

that I mean, that we make an offer to our adversary for them to settle the matter in the private so that restitution to both parties' former status is achieved – as closely as is possible given the circumstances.

We begin by outlining the case against them – by citing every breach of legislation that they've made, as well as throwing in some common and merchant law breaches.

This is a significant part of our offer as it informs them of what we now know, demonstrated by our evidence that we can prove beyond reasonable doubt. We cite everything with the clear statement that should they fail for the final time to act honourably in resolving the matter then we will progress to a claim against them that WILL be registered with the courts for adjudication. A significant part of this is to boldly inform them that it'll be *their* decision that influences the direction the matter will take from here.

All of this is a shot across their bow to demonstrate that we have multiple charges to bring against them and will likely gain merit for the case to proceed in the court. If they continue with their Goliath to our David stance, believing that we can't possibly win *any* case against them, and subsequently decline our offer – or even ignore us, then we'll have already and very specifically detailed what will happen next.

There's generally a price to be paid by anyone that breaches legislation and enriches themselves at our expense, as detailed extensively in reams of treatise by far more knowledgeable people than I, so on that basis alone we need to evaluate our course of action based on what we feel most aggrieved about, and what presents as the path of least resistance to reach our remedy. Very conveniently, that path is laid out by civil procedure rules and legislation.

The bank (if it is a bank we're going after) knows our intent and has already seen the difficulties inherent in answering our claims from the process in the first book and the near-impossibility presented in formulating a satisfactory response.

We set up the scenario carefully and methodically to create the perfect trap with which to gain the bank's confession of the facts. We already have significant evidence for the case in the letters they send, and the process from the first book (The Title is Unimportant) has already cemented their capitulation, generated their confession to the facts, and produced the smoking gun we need for the next stage. The Affidavit we served on them and their subsequent failure to respond is strong supporting evidence to their confession to the facts.

The bank will *always* maintain their aloof standing and, as has been proven time and again, position themselves as being far beyond reachable regarding matters of accountability. And yet, the news is filled with bank prosecutions, fines and sanctions as a result of being caught with less-than-honourable intentions. Unfortunately for our adversaries, law is law, and no one is above it (so we're told) and so a 'hit list' is required as the basis from which to launch our genuine claims. Our strength in this matter is very simply, that

241

the 'system' cannot be seen publicly to have failed. So as long as we observe *their* rules and the appropriate procedure for bringing a perfected claim to the court, then we should meet with our planned remedy.

The 'hit list' comprises many things that we could go at them for, but we must keep it within the bounds of what we can realistically achieve. The stories of never-ending court battles fill the media, and the bank could keep us fighting in court with them for years theoretically, so we must concentrate on realistic goals and stick to the points that are supported with strong evidence.

Any one of the charges we cite could be significantly damaging to them, but some are more readily useable than others, and that's primarily because we don't necessarily have to do anything other than report the bank to their governing bodies for things to happen.

Our goal is financial remedy - a settlement figure that reverses the monetary damage and returns each party to their former state as it was before we engaged – a process called *Restitution*. In the commercial system the only remedy that can be achieved is of a financial nature, and so that's where we're headed.

We also and quite significantly, require a full retraction of any and all judgments registered with the credit file agencies, and that also extends to instruction for every interloper that was assigned to collect on the account.

We're aiming at a clean sweep of the entire credit file and a restoration of our standing.

It's important at this stage for those on this path to fully understand that the bank will never be able to recall our security instrument and hand it back to us. No matter how hard they might try, that instrument has likely passed through dozens of 'owners' on its trading journey. Tracing orders can be implemented to track it down (done at the bank's expense) but in all likelihood, the security is long gone down the chasm of the market and even if it were found there would likely be quite a few investors that bought it in good faith and the can of worms that would be opened up from there is mind-boggling. In any case, were it found and returned to us it would be defaced by bankers marks and trading code – which is NOT what we gave them OR what we want back.

And to clarify – the reason for our getting back the original document is so that we can file it – or destroy it (and stop anyone else from trading our energy.)

What all of that means, is that there will *always* be restitution due to us as a function of rebalancing that loss / defacement.

And then there's all of the unscrupulous behaviour that occurred afterwards that needs to be accounted for, as the bank proceeded to make demands and veiled threats, collect our money, and generally behave as though they had a right to do whatever they wanted, and that is going to cost them.

So, the main thrust of this work is to reach *private settlement* with the bank. Getting back our security is really of no consequence to us – as compared with the bank doing the right thing and exchanging our energy / signature for the current commercial tokens as should have been the case from the outset!

Any sound mind reading this will already have realised that the bank paying up, reversing their errors, and then slipping quietly out the back door is an infinitely better prospect, as compared with the likelihood of becoming a front & center media focus in the courtroom and social media, and so the plan is that they will most likely view this strategy as a considerably less expensive outcome all round.

So we offer them the path of least resistance from the beginning, and we do that by citing everything in our case and demonstrating exactly what the legislation & common law says about the penalties they can look forwards to if they'd rather do it the hard way.

We illustrate the likely punishments they'll face - particularly the CEO and executive officers (and we name them wherever possible) if the court finds against them, including the effects this will have on their business in the future i.e. FCA, FSA suspension, downgraded credit rating, hefty fines and potential criminal prosecutions at the executive level. Remember the companies Act that requires them to set aside their own interests in favour of the company's well-being and sustainability? The worst-case scenario for these executives could be jail time in addition to huge losses for the bank in restitution payments, and that scenario could only ever grow into a behemoth situation once social media got hold of it.

This is all shaping up into a very serious matter and isn't something to be taken lightly from any perspective. The bottom line is that if we begin the process, we had better be prepared to go through with it - to the end. And yes, that sounds a bit dramatic, but we're injured right? We've suffered losses and are commercially f***ed for the immediate future, along with many thousands of others on a daily basis since at least the last 300 years. That's currently a LOT of people wanting the situation resolving.

This book contains the tools to correct that imbalanced situation but the process isn't for doubters. If the bank / DCA, or court detect any hesitation or holes in understanding, they will call our bluff – because that's the nature of this arena. As stated in the 'Title', this is a game of 'cahoonas'.

All of the impositions inflicted upon us so far, like damaged credit ratings and servitude where none is legally required, by institutions that are supposed to be prohibited from acting in such a way, were done predominantly because we smelled a rat and called them out on it.

So we make them an offer to settle in the private, but not before we've shown them that we have the means (and balls) to settle it in the courts if that's their preference.

For those feint of heart types who may be now getting despondent about the prospect of appearing in court and taking them on - relax. None of this is to say that we *will* go to court, but our adversary needs to know that we *can*, if we choose. They might double down on their actions and ignore us, and it wouldn't be the first time, but we have options.

One of those options would be reporting them to all of their governing bodies – FSA, ICO and FCA to name three, and include all of our evidence to show the multiple breaches of legislation by the bank.

At that point it's out of our hands and we're unlikely to get anything by way of remedy funds (although it isn't ruled out, as compensation rules still apply) BUT the bank will be subjected to investigation and suffer significant repercussions - not least when the governing body publishes their reports.

I can already hear the detractors saying "but the overseers of the banking monopoly will just be paid off to state there's no contravention of the rules", and yes, that's entirely possible and somewhat likely, but if it gets that far and things don't happen, despite our evidence, then we go higher and make claims on the directors of the governing bodies for their failure to adhere and apply law / legislation in the matter. There is *always* remedy – we just need to find it.

All of this can be escalated indefinitely to the point where it becomes necessary for somebody in a position of authority to act within the law or face significant numbers of people bringing class actions against the establishment itself. Class actions are VERY hard to ignore and are fairly easy to assemble nowadays thanks to social media.

At the end of the day - if it were me in the hot-seat facing all of this, I know which way I'd prefer, especially if I had the ability to offer an NDA for the deal and use it to create the payoff at no cost to myself, retract a few judgments and dig myself out of a hole quietly!

So we calculate our direct and indirect losses sustained by doing business with them. The money they've taken - based on the face value of our created security instrument, the money they sold it for (under unjust enrichment), the interest they made (unjust enrichment), the aggravation and anxiety they caused when writing to us (harm and loss), and then we can look at the sheer audacity of what they've done.

The theft of our property, damage to our commercial standing, demands, breach of data protection, misrepresentation, breach of public trust etc. - all of it.

At that point we arrive at a figure. And then we multiply that by SEVEN because the Bible says 'when the thief is caught he will be made to pay sevenfold'. We use Biblical reference purely because the Bible and other Holy books are in every courtroom, and the reason for that, is that they are all commercial manuals for conducting oneself properly in commerce, and this is absolutely a commercial claim.

Don't get too excited at this stage (well maybe a little bit). Restitution awards from the court come in at roughly 7% of the claimed amount, and that's why we inflate our charges pursuant to Biblically recommended levels.

We must also factor in the level of *tort* we endured in all of this, and because no one can tell us what our pain (or our time) is worth to us, only WE can decide what that value is.

This is IF we go the reporting to their governing bodies and / or court route.

In the event of their failure to settle on the basis of potential further action, then we must pick our next battle very carefully.

We have options of registering the case with the courts or reporting to governing bodies OR we can follow the devastating (to them) commercial lien route.

If we decide to pursue them in the courts, we have to select the most appropriate claims or claim by identifying the best scenario for a relatively easy win, and stick to that path no matter what. There's no gain to be had from issuing a case that doesn't have a straight route to the goal. Jumping around between different claims is of no use to anyone when it comes to nailing it down BUT we can make mention of everything we have on them as a frame of reference to illustrate the character of our adversary.

We have a good amount of breaches to choose from but some of them will present difficulties to achieve without an arduous fight, and we absolutely MUST follow due process as it applies to our particular route. As it stands, many breaches have their own pre-action protocols for claiming and must be followed to the letter - IF we are to be taken seriously. There's no success to be found in bringing a frivolous claim to the court that hasn't observed the correct route of getting there, as defence lawyers will have an easy time of taking it apart.

As a general guide, before commencement of proceedings, the court will expect the parties to have exchanged sufficient information to:

(a) understand each other's position

(b) make decisions about how to proceed

(c) try to settle the issues without proceedings

(d) consider a form of Alternative Dispute Resolution (ADR) to assist with settlement

(e) support the efficient management of those proceedings and

(f) reduce the costs of resolving the dispute.

We must work with what we have at hand in terms of our evidence, and it must all be produced. A significant part of this is the cured Affidavit, which, if standing as unrebutted, forms a full confession by the bank of the facts in the matter. That alone *should* be the beginning and end of the case but we will produce more. There's nothing quite like a sizeable body of evidence against the defendant to remove any doubts as to their actions.

The first and most important part of the whole process is to void the original contract the bank believe they have with us. Voiding the contract and showing that it was never legitimate in the first place, produces an immediate cataclysm for the bank, as they cannot claim any legal justification for what they have been doing for the life of the account. They already know all this, and that's the primary reason they hardly go to court with a claim, but we need to put that on the record from the outset. Any objections to that can be easily countered by asking them to prove us wrong – "please produce the proof that a verified legitimate contract exists between the parties by providing sight of the original issue paperwork".

To void the contract we again invite them to validate their position for the final time, via the production of evidence to support the legally required principle that consideration was produced by them in the first instance – a precise demonstration that they actually brought something of value, that was theirs, to the agreement. We want to see all of the details showing the movement of 'money' from their side over to ours.

We ask that they produce the original agreement (the security) that formed OUR consideration to them. They are required to keep this until the day we settle the account (loan or credit) and redeem our property, at which point it must be returned to us unmarked.

We ask them to demonstrate that the bank did not treat our document as cash – which will be difficult, as banking codes actually state that that is precisely what it is treated as.

We ask them where it was shown that they provided full disclosure of the material facts.

We ask them to deny on the record that:

1. we created a security instrument,

2. that they sold it for profit

3. that we funded the credit advanced to us

4. that they opened an insurance policy to protect themselves in the event of our failure to pay

5. that they charged us interest on our own money

6. that they sold the alleged account to a DCA for further profit

Their total failure to produce consideration, as well as meet any of the other required components for a legally binding contract at the start of the relationship, is something that's impossible to rectify at this stage. They can never prove that they lent something to us – because they didn't, and the record will show that.

They also can't do anything about their failure to sign

off on the contract with TWO human signatures at executive level, because on all the *copies* they have available, there is usually only one signature present, and that is ours!

So the point of this exercise is to gain their full confession and agreement to the facts in the matter, at which point the game is up. This was all covered in the Title is Unimportant and produces a document that stands as the truth in the matter. At this point a child could demonstrate that the contract they assume exists between us is an absolute fantasy.

To recap:

Void the contract

1. Void the original contract by citing all their failures under contracting law

2. Get their tacit confession via Affidavit of Claim

Cite losses, impositions and harm caused

1. Loss of our property (the security instrument)

2. Loss of our *re*payments paid

3. Loss of interest payments paid

4. Loss of commercial standing

5. Difficulty or impossibility of obtaining further credit

6. Difficulty in contracting with other businesses

7. Undue / unwarranted stress caused by bank

8. Unauthorised sharing of our personal data

9. Unauthorised contact from 3rd parties

Specify the legislation that was breached

1. Cite the Acts they've breached and the applicable sections

Make the case for prosecution

1. List our schedule that we'll be claiming in court.

2. Cite appropriate legislation to support our claim(s).

3. Cite the governing bodies we'll be reporting to

Present the offer

1. Offer the out-of-court settlement under a non-disclosure scheme

2. Advise that this will settle and close the matter and that no further action will ensue once the parties have been restored to their original position.

Pre-Action Protocol

As stated earlier, the court *expects* us to have followed the guidelines. Failure to observe them precisely will result in the defendant having an easy time of dismantling our case on grounds of failure in due process.

Before our claim is even heard the case will fall at the first hurdle if due process has not been followed. Failure in due process is an angle that's been used personally in several cases to dismantle claims made against myself and friends. The claimants, often despite having legal teams at their disposal, regularly fail to adhere to due process despite a comprehensive understanding of its necessity. Once the fault is pointed out, it's up to the Judge whether or not they allow the case to proceed on a flawed basis, and if they do overlook the fault, it doesn't magically repair the claim.

Pre-action protocols are specific to each type of claim and are generally a series of 'fair play' maneuvers designed to bring the dispute to resolution without involving the court wherever possible. They are crucial to the claim gaining the required merit to be heard in the court.

If the protocols fail to produce a resolution in the

private then the court will likely take the case if merit is granted.

They typically go as follows:

1. Letter of Claim

A formal letter of claim is sent to the defendant outlining the details of the claim – much the same as our offer letter does. It covers legal basis, facts, and the remedy sought. The defendant is given say, fourteen days to respond.

2. Initiation of Court Proceedings

If the defendant fails to acknowledge service of the letter of claim and or doesn't enter into discussion to resolve the matter, the claim is escalated to the court.

The court in which the claim is filed depends on the nature and value of the claim. Small claims (up to £10,000) are usually dealt with in the County Court or online through small claims fast track service, while higher-value or more complex cases may be brought before the High Court or specialised courts.

3. Issuing the Claim

To start court proceedings, the claimant completes the relevant claim form (such as the N1 form) and submits it to the court. The claim form contains details about the parties, the nature of the claim, and the relief sought. A fee is usually payable, which varies based on the claim's value.

4. Serving the Claim

Once the claim form is issued by the court, it needs to be served on the defendant. Service methods include personal service (delivery by hand), first-class post, or other permitted means. Proof of service must be provided to the court.

5. Acknowledgment of Service and Defense

Upon receiving the claim form, the defendant must file an acknowledgment of service with the court within a specific timeframe. This includes a section detailing whether they intend to defend the claim or concede. If they intend to defend the claim they must file a defense within the given time limit, outlining their version of events and legal arguments.

6. Directions and Case Management

The court may issue directions to manage the case effectively. This could involve setting deadlines for exchanging evidence, filing witness statements, or attending case management conferences. The court may also encourage parties to consider alternative dispute resolution methods like mediation.

7. Disclosure and Evidence

The parties are typically required to disclose relevant documents to each other during the disclosure stage. They also exchange witness statements, expert reports (if necessary), and any other evidence supporting their case.

8. Trial / Hearing

If the case proceeds to trial, both parties present their arguments, evidence, and witnesses before a Judge. The Judge then makes a decision based on the law and the facts presented.

9. Judgment and Enforcement

Following the trial, the court delivers a judgment, which sets out the legal outcome of the case. If the claimant is successful, the court may award damages or other appropriate remedies. If enforcement is required to recover the awarded amount, further legal steps may be necessary.

Non-Litigation

If we just want to hit the bank as hard as possible for their actions, we can simply provide their governing bodies with all of our evidence showing that they made several serious breaches to the legislation. We also make a point that we want to be informed of their actions and the punishment resulting from their investigations and

actions to correct the record.
So the steps to getting our remedy are as follows:

1. Send the bank an Affidavit of Claim to set up their confession of the facts in the matter. (We should have already completed this stage from The Title is Unimportant)

2. Send the bank our acceptance of their full confession and agreement to the facts via their failure to rebut the Affidavit. Include our offer for them to settle in the private based on all citations of the legislation they've breached including a proviso that in the event of their failure we will commence proceedings through the courts and / or report them to relevant governing bodies.

3. Should the bank fail to accept our offer (expected) either;

    (i)   Begin the process of registering their behaviour to relevant authorities

    (ii)   Begin the process of registering the case with the court

    (iii) Begin the commercial lien process on both the bank AND the respective offenders individually

4. Once the lien is cured, issue notices of default, register them with credit reference agencies, and engage the court to instruct bailiffs to collect our remedy.

The commercial lien process is an entirely separate and considerable subject, and far more than the scope of this book allows. Plenty of information can be found online and in many legal treatise'. There may be a Debt Ninjas foray into it as some point in the future.

Obviously the easiest path for all concerned is for the bank to just settle in the private, after all, it doesn't cost them anything to resolve the matter by producing a credit to our bank account – because they'll get another security instrument when we sign off on the Non Disclosure Agreement. It also doesn't cost them anything to retract all of their judgments on our credit file as part of the deal.

The immediate problem the bank will have is that they'll know we've done our homework and *could* get this into the court and give them a hard time *very* publicly. And just to be clear, they WILL consider every dirty trick in the book to protect themselves against this action including defamation, threats with malice's and even buying a Judge or two. They'll also know that this situation isn't easily defendable without them having to *lie* and double down on their risk of being caught operating a fraud.

The bank (or whoever) is on shifting sands in all of this but you can be assured of several things if the court is successfully engaged:

(i)   The Judge will have likely been bought.

(ii)   You will have to appear in the court as a litigant in person – because you cannot trust a lawyer as they are already under a prior oath to the court - not us.

(iii)   The case will attract a lot of attention, both from the Public and the media. You will likely become (in)famous (Watch "The Man Who Sued God") as this will be the first time an action of this nature has ever made it into a public gallery and, win or lose the case, the bank will face heavy losses, through an overnight erosion of public faith in the entire banking system.

(iv)   Should WE lose the case, after all of our due diligence, being guided by pre-action protocols and the legislation itself, it would produce a shockwave that'd ripple through the entire legislative system and could potentially expose it as a sham against the people, operating as a thin veneer of justice purely for those in the higher echelons of privilege. The ramifications of *that* scenario are wide-ranging and hugely damaging to the establishment - and that can't be allowed to happen (not just yet).

Part of the trepidation for the bank regarding a court case is the potential risk of them losing *very publicly*. It's their second biggest fear (after being forced to produce their ledgers) and by rights, (at least in a rational mind) that scenario should produce a situation where common sense ought to prevail in the CEO's office regarding risk management when considering our offer. Personally, I would bite the bullet and capitulate to what's being requested - but then I'm not a banker, don't roll people daily, and have little interest in operating deceitfully.

Whichever way all of this goes, there's only one scenario that allows the bank to continue its operations without too much inconvenience (for the time being) and that's the private settlement route.

Ultimately, the writing is on the wall for the banks as they currently exist, and the only thing that determines how quickly the game ends, is which option they want to take.

Chapter Twenty

Template

Letter Before Claim - Bank

As I said in 'The Title is Unimportant', templates are not the be all and end all when it comes to correspondence with these organisations. It would be unfair and unreasonable to expect a copy & paste exercise to produce our overnight freedom from those that would have our energy (and commercial tokens) in a single shot.

Templates are for guidance. To get you started with what to say correctly, and the form it must follow to be a coherent and serious document. That they do set our opponents back on their heels is one thing – as can be evidenced by their only defense to them being a weak statement about the use of templates from the internet not being acceptable forms of communication (while simultaneously responding in every case by sending a template letter of their own!?)

The focus of the templates is to guide. They are to lay out the flow of our response in a linear way thereby avoiding rambling & repetition and making a clear statement for our case.

Use them to assist your personalised communication. Alter them to suit your situation but don't change the main points as they're designed precisely to back our opponent into the corner, hopefully where they'll be damned if they do and damned if they don't.

Here then, is the first of the new templates that have been designed to fire a shot across the bow of the bank and prepare them for the next stage, which is to get our restitution and force the credit file correction.

As usual, for ease of alteration the word docs can be accessed by dropping an email to info@debt-ninjas.com and including your proof of purchase. Once you have them you'll see the obvious sections you need to change for your situation are highlighted in red.

Coimbatore Sundararajan Venkatakrishnan
CEO Barclaycard
1 Churchill Place
London
England
E14 5HP

P Michael Yates
****
****
****
****
[Postcode]

Ref 0001 2000 3000 4000

LETTER BEFORE CLAIM

STATEMENT OF FACT
NOTICE OF FAULT AND OPPORTUNITY TO CURE

Notice to Agent is Notice to Principal,
Notice to Principal is Notice to Agent

Dear Coimbatore Sundararajan Venkatakrishnan, please read the following Notice carefully. It is a Notice NOT a complaint or dispute and therefore should not be treated as such.

265

Legal Maxims

Ignorance of the Law is no defence.

Truth as a valid statement of reality is Sovereign in commerce.

An un-rebutted Affidavit stands as truth in commerce.

An un-rebutted Affidavit is acted upon as the judgement in commerce.

Silence comprises agreement in commerce, equity, admiralty, Lex Mercatoria and public policy, as he who does not deny when he has the opportunity, admits the facts presented to him.

All men shall have a remedy by due course of the law. If a remedy does not exist or if the existing remedy has been subverted, then one may create a remedy for them selves and endow it with credibility by expressing it in their Affidavit.

Except for a jury, it is also a fatal offence for any person, even a judge, to impair or to expunge without a counter Affidavit, any Affidavit or any commercial process based upon an Affidavit.

A foreclosure by a summary judgement (without Jury), without a commercial bond, is a violation of commercial law.

An official (officer of the court, policeman, etc.) must demonstrate that he is individually bonded in order to use a summary process.

The official, who impairs, debauches, voids or abridges an obligation of contract or the effect of a commercial lien without proper cause becomes a lien debtor, and his property becomes forfeited as a pledge to secure the lien.

It is against the law for a judge to summarily remove, dismiss, dissolve or diminish a commercial lien. Only the lien claimant or a jury can dissolve a commercial lien.

This Notice is served in compliance with and in respect of due process and pre-action protocols, as required and set forth in British legal jurisprudence. It is to make efforts to settle a matter in a timely and appropriate manner and, wherever possible, avoid the need for engagement of the courts as adjudicator.

The evidence in my possession demonstrates several clear breaches of United Kingdom legislation by Barclaycard under the leadership of Coimbatore Sundararajan Venkatakrishnan, who's Public Liability Insurance (bond) will be drawn upon to satisfy the claimed restitution.

My Affidavit of Claim was served on Coimbatore Sundararajan Venkatakrishnan, and Barclaycard on the

24th Octember, 2094 and stands as unrebutted – the truth in the matter under the legal maxim that 'an unrebutted Affidavit stands as the truth in commerce'. That cured document now serves as testament to the full and final confession to the facts by Coimbatore Sundararajan Venkatakrishnan, and Barclaycard.

My Affidavit outlined several actions undertaken by Barclaycard over a period of time during which I made sincere attempts to resolve the situation with an alleged loan / credit facility that was purported to be lent to me by Barclaycard. The subsequent failure by Barclaycard to respond appropriately to my claims by providing a satisfactory rebuttal with full proofs of claim has now resulted in the perfected claim as being the truth in the matter under "He who fails to deny – accepts".

I now intend to resolve the matter and bring this situation to a close, and part of that process is to claim restitution from Barclaycard via Coimbatore Sundararajan Venkatakrishnan, in addition to demanding that my credit file containing several erroneous entries made by Barclaycard AND their third parties, be expunged of ALL entries arising out of this matter.

For the record, and ease of reference, the following are charges applicable for dubious acts committed against me by Barclaycard under the leadership of Coimbatore Sundararajan Venkatakrishnan, during the period covering our alleged business relationship.

1. Deception
2. Failure to disclose
3. Misappropriation
4. Misrepresentation
5. Concealment
6. Commercial damage
7. Defamation
8. Embezzlement
9. Data protection breach
10. Theft
11. Unjust enrichment
12. Cybercrime
13. Racketeering
14. Insurance fraud
15. Harassment
16. Tax evasion

These charges form the basis of my legal action against Barclaycard and I fully understand and accept that some of the charges cited may be more difficult than others to apply in a legal sense. Consequently I will select the claims most suited to an easier resolution – the low hanging fruit as it were, whilst citing all charges as reference to illustrate the precise nature of the character of Barclaycard under Coimbatore Sundararajan Venkatakrishnan's, leadership.

The exact legislation that has been breached by Barclaycard is as follows:

1. The Fraud Act 2006

2. The Criminal Finances Act 2017

3. The Torts Act 1977

4. The Bank of England and Financial Services Act 2016

5. The Modern Slavery Act 2015

6. The Defamation Act 2013

7. The Financial Services Act 2012

8. The Misrepresentation Act 1967

9. The Malicious Communications Act 1988

10. The Data Protection Act 2018

11. The Protection from Harassment Act 1997

12. The Theft Act 1968

13. The Bills of Exchange Act 1882

14. The Proceeds of Crime Act 2002

You may be aware at this stage (I'm quite sure you are), that your failure to enforce the contract you believe exists between us, is very simply because there never was any contract in existence that could be enforced. That fact is now self-evident and fully confessed by Barclaycard via failure to rebut my Affidavit and correct the record. It no doubt forms a significant part of the bank's reluctance to move the case into the courts, and fosters the preference for selling the failed account to a debt collection agency after moving it off-ledger.
The obvious failures to adhere to basic contracting pillars (required as a basis for ALL contracting) are as numerous as they are obvious and are sufficient to render my claim meritorious.

For the avoidance of any doubt I again invite you for a final time to prove your claim that there exists / existed a bona fide contract between Barclaycard and myself. You can do this simply by providing me with a photograph of the original contract signed by TWO executive directors per the Bills of Exchange Act 1882, and detailing my own signature, along with full accounting detailing your consideration, as required under contracting rules, thereby producing the required proof that you did not securitise my property.

There now follows a detailed summary of the legislation breached by Barclaycard during the course of the alleged agreement between us:

Deception

Barclaycard has failed at every opportunity to disclose what has now been established on the record as a failure to disclose:

- that I created a security instrument / promissory note

- that the bank accepted my created promissory note as cash

- that the note was used to fund the 'loan / credit'

- that the note was added to the bank's ledger as an asset

- that the bank sold it on the securities market as original issue

- that the bank engaged an insurance policy to cover potential failure of the account

- that the bank was engaged in a conflict of interests

- that the bank made profit on sale of said security

- that the bank did not move any money / credit from their own assets into my credit account

- that the bank collected monthly payments in service of the alleged debt

- that the bank charged interest on the alleged debt (Usury)

The above charges are already confessed by Barclaycard due to failure to respond / rebut my Affidavit and form a breach of the Fraud Act 2006 by fraudulent misrepresentation, fraud by non-disclosure, and fraud by concealment.

As a result of these actions I have suffered damages.

Defamation

Barclaycard has engaged in a breach of the Defamation Act 2013 due to its reporting of my alleged breach of contract with them at the credit reference agencies, when it can be demonstrated positively that no contract existed that could have been breached by myself.

Barclaycard also incited third parties to commit a breach of the Act by informing them incorrectly of my standing regarding breach of contract.

Plausible deniability is not acceptable as a defense for this breach as Barclaycard were fully aware from the outset that no contract-between-the-parties exists as can be amply evidenced by their failure to produce a valid contract despite repeated requests.

As a result of these actions I have suffered damages.

This charge forms a breach of The Defamation Act 2013.

Negligence

Barclaycard has failed routinely to respond to sincere and forthright questions about this matter and have stated on several occasions that they "*will not, and have no obligation to answer said questions*". This standing demonstrates *secrecy* and is not permitted under FCA rules.

Barclaycard has abandoned its *duty of care* (as is required under legislation) and has committed a *breach of duty* with regard to investigating my claims to the fullest extent, and by failing to perform their obligations in a competent and diligent manner.

As a result of these actions I have suffered damages.

This charge will be submitted under a breach of the Torts Act 1977.

Malicious Communications

Since no legitimate contract was ever in place between the parties (Barclaycard and myself) regarding a credit facility, it therefore follows that ALL communications received from Barclaycard containing requests for payment, threats of collection activity or any mail of any description are malicious in nature and form a comprehensive breach of the Malicious Communications Act 1988.

As a result of these actions I have suffered damages.

Misappropriation

My created promissory note (security instrument) was taken by Barclaycard and subsequently sold, payments from my account were taken to service a non-existent debt, interest applied to a non-existent debt, and my property sold without disbursement of profits to myself (the original issuer). These actions breach several acts namely:

1. The Theft Act 1968

2. The Data Protection Act 2018

3. The Fraud Act 2006

4. The Consumer Rights Act 2015

And of course, common law principles such as the law of equity and the doctrine of unjust enrichment will be applied.

As a result of these actions I have suffered damages.

Misrepresentation

At the outset of my interaction with Barclaycard, no statement was made to me that reflected the true nature of the engagement. At no point did Barclaycard inform me:

- that I created a security instrument / promissory note

- that my creation would be used to fund the credit / loan

- that Barclaycard would sell my property on the securities markets and keep the profits

- that Barclaycard would engage an insurance policy around the account thus effectively taking a hedge position *against* my ability to service the monthly payments

- that Barclaycard was operating a conflict of interests

- that Barclaycard produced NO consideration under the 'agreement'

- that Barclaycard would fail to sign the contract appropriately per the Bills of Exchange Act 1882

- that the contract was void from the outset and thus meaningless

- that Barclaycard would go on to breach several sections of UK legislation in their attempts to pursue me for collection of an illusory debt under a fictional contract

- that I would be expected to endure several commercial impositions as a result of doing business with Barclaycard

Barclaycard DID inform me of the following:

- that they were 'lending' money

- that interest would be applied to the amount to 'cover their losses'

- that the agreement was a legally binding contract

- that serious repercussions would be applied to my financial standing in the event of my failure to adhere to the contract

I was assured by Barclaycard that the process was above-board and legitimate. I have since learned that this was not the case and, had I been appraised of the situation beforehand, i.e. had Barclaycard NOT employed deception from the outset, had been honest and upfront about the situation, I would NOT have chosen to do business with them. This is a clear and self-evident reliance on misrepresentation to attract business via concealment of the facts.

This constitutes a comprehensive breach of the Misrepresentation Act 1967.

As a result of these actions I have suffered damages.

Concealment

Fraud by concealment or fraudulent concealment was employed by Barclaycard from the outset whereby false statements and misrepresentations were used throughout the 'agreement' process. This was done either deliberately or innocently. Information that I have an absolute right to know under the principle of full disclosure and under obligation by Barclaycard, was entirely absent from the process.

This comprises a breach of the Fraud Act 2006.

As a result of these actions I have suffered damages.

Commercial Damage

As a direct result of doing business with Barclaycard I have sustained damage to my financial status. Through process of automatic reporting by Barclaycard to the credit file agencies, my commercial standing has been impacted considerably. The well-settled obligation within contract law, that ALL processes be halted, whether automatic or not, in the event of a contract dispute or the discovery of a fault in the agreement, until such time as the situation is resolved, has been fully abandoned by Barclaycard as they proceeded to inflict damage without due cause despite my contact with them to raise the issue.

In addition I have also been subject to coercion in making payments including interest to service an illegitimate debt as a direct result of Barclaycard's actions in concealment.

This comprises a breach of several legislative areas notably:

- The Unfair Contract Terms Act 1977

- The Data Protection Act 2018

- The Fraud Act 2006

And Tort law (Common Law)

As a result of these actions I have suffered damages.

Defamation

Barclaycard registered information with the credit reference agencies that I am a bad debtor – a bad credit risk. This position is now known to be wholly incorrect and current registries are false and misleading. In the absence of due diligence Barclaycard abandoned their duty of care and proceeded to make remarks and statements that are false. As creditor in the first instance, my standing is impeccable and will always be so. The credit file is yet more evidence of malfeasance by Barclaycard.

This comprises a comprehensive breach of the Defamation Act 2013.

As a result of these actions I have suffered damages.

Embezzlement

Barclaycard stole my security instrument, sold it on the markets, failed to disburse the profits with me (as the originator) and concealed the process.

This comprises a breach of the Theft Act 1978, specifically sections 1, 4, and 17.

As a result of these actions I have suffered damages.

Data Protection Breach

Barclaycard collected, stored, manipulated, and disseminated my personal data from the outset of the alleged credit agreement. Since no legitimate contract exists between the parties and despite repeated attempts to view said insisted contract, it therefore follows that there is NO authority under which Barclaycard can rely upon for holding, processing, and sharing my personal data in their database.

Barclaycard at no time had any legitimate authority for the use of my private and confidential information, and this fact produces a comprehensive breach of the Data Protection Act 2018.

As a result of these actions I have suffered damages.

Theft

Barclaycard stole my promissory note in the first instance and proceeded to collect monthly repayments plus interest. These actions are described adequately in UK legislation and fall under the Theft Act 1968.

As a result of these actions I have suffered damages.

Unjust Enrichment

Barclaycard have unfairly benefitted from my property and actions through concealment of the facts and by failure to disclose. The theft of my promissory note and its subsequent sale on the market along with my monthly payments plus interest to service the alleged debt have generated unethical / unjust revenue for the bank at my expense.

This action will produce a claim for disgorgement of profits under restitution principles.

As a result of these actions I have suffered damages.
Cybercrime

Barclaycard used online forms to collect my personal and private information as part of their alleged contracting process during the agreement stage. No part of an electronic agreement or 'signature' complies with the Bills of Exchange Act 1882 or the Companies Act 71,

2008, and fails comprehensively to meet the well-settled pillars of proper contract formation. The contract was never launched in any legal sense despite Barclaycard maintaining false assurances that a valid contract *was* in place between the parties. Through the online application process, Barclaycard are breaching the Data Protection Act 2018 by collecting private information under misrepresentation.

This action will be filed under breach of the Data Protection Act 2018.

As a result of these actions I have suffered damages.

Racketeering

Barclaycard completed an alleged credit application with myself, during which time they issued false statements, employed misdirection, embezzlement, concealment, misrepresentation, misappropriation, deception, and negligence. These actions lead to a situation whereby I was forced to endure harassment, defamation, commercial damage, DPA breaches, unjust enrichment, theft, malicious communications and other damages not limited to psychological harm.
This behaviour by Barclaycard is not an isolated incident it is BANK POLICY and occurs every day to many people throughout the world. The situation has been clearly defined in legal terms as Racketeering.

This action will be filed under the Proceeds of Crime Act 2002 and the Bribery Act 2010.

As a result of these actions I have suffered damages.

Insurance fraud

Barclaycard, upon receiving my online application for 'credit' subsequently implemented an insurance policy around the new account to cover them against my potential future inability to service the alleged debt. This is a direct conflict of interests as it presents the bank with a win-win scenario whichever future event happens and offers further gains at my expense.

Also as Barclaycard did not advance any credit or assets belonging to themselves, the insured amount was / is fictional as no property insured belonged to Barclaycard.

This action will be filed under the Fraud Act 2006, the Insurance Act 2015, the Proceeds of Crime Act 2002, and the Financial Services and Markets Act 2000.

As a result of these actions I have suffered damages.

Harassment

Barclaycard engaged in sustained efforts at communication in the form of physical letters to my private address as well as emails to my private email address, making requests / demands for me to pay monies to service an alleged debt that was claimed by them to be subject to a legitimate contract between the parties. Barclaycard also made telephone calls advising that the account would soon be moved to their 'collections team' for further action, with an inference that a wrong had been committed by myself, and that I should expect unpleasant action in the near future, as well as damage to my commercial standing via negative credit file entries.

Any form of contact from an entity unwilling to respond appropriately to a series of inquiry letters, and in the absence of a bona fide contractual relationship as its basis, is harassment - especially contact of a threatening nature.

This matter will be dealt with under the Malicious Communications Act 1988.

As a result of these actions I have suffered damages.

Tax Evasion

Barclaycard traded my security instrument on the markets as original issue. Clearly, my created promissory note is NOT original issue by Barclaycard – it is MINE. Barclaycard is not able to create anything, being a fictional entity and a registered corporation. An investigation into whether Barclaycard pays any due taxes on profits accrued via trading of notes will be initiated in due course.

Summary

Barclaycard, under the direction of Coimbatore Sundararajan Venkatakrishnan has committed multiple breaches of UK legislation and continues to do so as a matter of bank policy. This behaviour leads to harm and loss to every client / victim of Barclaycard.

These breaches are as evident as they are common and must, by virtue of fairness and commercial good faith be halted immediately. Several attempts at correcting this matter have been made by myself and all have failed. This failure speaks volumes about Barclaycard and Coimbatore Sundararajan Venkatakrishnan and their unwillingness / inability to investigate properly cited faults and failures in their operation and has steered the course for this action.

Offer

The charges cited within this Notice are fully supported by evidence and will be used against the bank to secure restitution and correction of the record if no agreement can be reached. There are several options available for the resolution of this matter:

1. Barclaycard via Coimbatore Sundararajan Venkatakrishnan makes an apology settlement in the private to me, to produce full remedy, in addition to retracting all credit file entries made during the course of this matter. This also includes instruction to all 3rd parties after-the-fact to perform a similar retraction of credit file entries.

285

Remedy has been set at a conservative £2m and will produce correction and full and final settlement of the matter in the private. A Non Disclosure agreement, if required, will be duly signed.

2. Barclaycard via Coimbatore Sundararajan Venkatakrishnan will be cited in a private suit for several charges that will have been predetermined to have the best chance of success in claiming remedy and produce correction of my status.

3. Barclaycard and Coimbatore Sundararajan Venkatakrishnan with all executive level persons will be reported to governing bodies and regulatory agencies which will include copies of all evidence submitted to produce a public enquiry into the actions of the bank towards its customers.

4. A class action will be served upon Barclaycard with Coimbatore Sundararajan Venkatakrishnan and all executive level persons, by approximately 1,600 people (likely more), in a collective suit against Barclaycard. This will undoubtedly become a public media situation and, succeed or fail, will likely create significant impact to the bank's reputation. For some idea of how this operates, a cursory study of the case between Pacific Gas & Electric VS the People of Hinkley, California, might serve to illustrate what is possible when many people come together with a common goal.

I expect your full co-operation in resolving this matter at this stage, and look forward to receiving your proposal within 28 (twenty eight) days of the date this Notice is received (confirmation by Royal Mail tracking). Failure to respond within the required timeframe will be met with immediate progression to the next phase with full prejudice.

Please note that NO extra time will be granted in this matter.

Sincerely

P Michael Yates

Chapter Twenty One

Template

Letter Before Claim DCA

Steven Edward Daws
Director PRA Group (UK) Limited
Level 11 Riverside House
2s Southwark Bridge Road
London
England
SE1 9HA

P Michael Yates
****
****
****
****
[Postcode]

Ref 0001 2000 3000 4000

14th Septober 2023

LETTER BEFORE CLAIM

STATEMENT OF FACT
NOTICE OF FAULT AND OPPORTUNITY TO CURE

Notice to Agent is Notice to Principal,
Notice to Principal is Notice to Agent

Dear Steven Edward Daws, please read the following Notice carefully. It is a Notice NOT a complaint or dispute and therefore should not be treated as such.

Legal Maxims

Ignorance of the Law is no defence.

Truth as a valid statement of reality is Sovereign in commerce.

An un-rebutted Affidavit stands as truth in commerce. An un-rebutted Affidavit is acted upon as the judgement in commerce.

Silence comprises agreement in commerce, equity, admiralty, Lex Mercatoria and public policy, as he who does not deny when he has the opportunity, admits the facts presented to him.

All men shall have a remedy by due course of the law.

If a remedy does not exist or if the existing remedy has been subverted, then one may create a remedy for them selves and endow it with credibility by expressing it in their Affidavit.

Except for a jury, it is also a fatal offence for any person, even a judge, to impair or to expunge without a counter Affidavit, any Affidavit or any commercial process based upon an Affidavit.

A foreclosure by a summary judgement (without Jury), without a commercial bond, is a violation of commercial law.

An official (officer of the court, policeman, etc.), must demonstrate that he is individually bonded in order to use a summary process.

The official, who impairs, debauches, voids or abridges an obligation of contract or the effect of a commercial lien without proper cause becomes a lien debtor, and his property becomes forfeited as a pledge to secure the lien.

It is against the law for a judge to summarily remove, dismiss, dissolve or diminish a commercial lien. Only the lien claimant or a jury can dissolve a commercial lien.

This Notice is served in compliance with and in respect of due process and pre-action protocols, as required and set forth in British legal jurisprudence. It is to make attempts to settle a matter in a timely and appropriate manner and wherever possible avoid the need for engagement of the courts as adjudicator.

The evidence in my possession demonstrates several clear breaches of United Kingdom legislation by PRA Group (UK) Limited under the leadership of Steven Edward Daws, who's Public Liability Insurance (bond) will be drawn upon to satisfy the claim.

My Affidavit of Claim was served on Coimbatore Sundararajan Venkatakrishnan of Barclaycard on the 24th October, 2094 and stands as unrebutted – the truth in the matter under the legal maxim 'an unrebutted Affidavit stands as the truth in commerce'. That cured document now serves as testament to the full confession to the facts by Coimbatore Sundararajan Venkatakrishnan and Barclaycard.

The actions undertaken by Barclaycard over a period of time during which I made sincere attempts to resolve the situation with an alleged loan / credit facility that was purported to be lent to me by Barclaycard are detailed. The subsequent failure by Barclaycard to respond appropriately to my claims by providing a satisfactory rebuttal with full proofs of claim has now resulted in the perfected claim as being the truth in the matter under the legal maxim "He who fails to deny – accepts".

This confession to the facts in the matter places Barclaycard in a position of having breached several significant sections of UK legislation. The position Barclaycard now finds itself in extends to PRA Group (UK) Limited, through association, as the entirety of PRA Group (UK) Limited's actions have been undertaken as a result of Barclaycard's fraudulent concealment of crucial facts in the matter when selling the non-existent debt to PRA Group (UK) Limited, OR by fraudulent concealment of the facts when engaging PRA Group (UK) Limited to act in the matter on behalf of the bank.

The situation at present is that I have endured numerous letters and contact attempts by PRA Group (UK) Limited under the direction of Steven Edward Daws which are in breach of several aspects of UK legislation.

The legislation breached by PRA group (UK) Limited is as follows:

1. The Fraud Act 2006

2. The Criminal Finances Act 2017

3. The Torts Act 1977

4. The Modern Slavery Act 2015

5. The Defamation Act 2013

6. The Financial Services Act 2012

7. The Misrepresentation Act 1967

8. The Malicious Communications Act 1988

9. The Data Protection Act 2018

10. The Protection from Harassment Act 1997

11. The Bills of Exchange Act 1882

12. The Proceeds of Crime Act 2002

13. The Bribery Act 2010

It has been breached by the following actions:

1. Deception
2. Failure to disclose
3. Misrepresentation
4. Concealment
5. Defamation
6. Data protection breach
7. Racketeering
8. Harassment

In addition to these charges there is the addition of attempted extortion.

Some of these charges form the basis of my legal action against Barclaycard and are also applicable to PRA Group (UK) Limited.

It is my intention to bring this situation to a close soon, and part of that process is to claim restitution from Barclaycard via Coimbatore Sundararajan Venkatakrishnan in addition to demanding that my credit file containing several erroneous entries made by Barclaycard AND their third parties, be expunged of ALL entries arising out of this matter and the record set straight.

PRA Group (UK) Limited has received my letter(s) in proximate response to inappropriate communications to myself and have comprehensively failed to respond in any manner proportionate to the situation.

It is on this basis that my claim will be made unless an appropriate settlement is made to a) expunge the record at the credit file agencies and b) make suitable remedy for the harm and loss (commercial damages) endured by myself as a result of PRA Group (UK) Limited's actions in this matter.

For the avoidance of any doubt I again invite you for a final time to prove your claim that there exists / existed a bona fide contract between Barclaycard and myself, PRA Group (UK) Limited and myself and / or, all three parties. You can do this simply by providing me with a photograph of the original contract signed by TWO executive directors per the Bills of Exchange Act 1882, and detailing my own signature, along with full accounting detailing Barclaycard's consideration-under-the-agreement, as required under contracting rules, along with the contract you believe exists between myself and PRA Group (UK) Limited, thereby producing the required proof of claim as is required under law.

There now follows a detailed summary of the legislation breached by PRA Group (UK) Limited in the course of contacting me:

Defamation

PRA Group (UK) Limited engaged in a breach of the Defamation Act 2013 due to its false reporting of my breach of alleged contract with them at the credit reference agencies, when it has been proven positively that no contract exists that could have been breached by myself. Barclaycard instructed third parties to pursue me for a fictitious debt thereby inciting PRA Group (UK) Limited to commit a breach of the Act by informing them incorrectly of my standing.

Plausible deniability is not acceptable as a defence for this breach, as PRA Group (UK) Limited were fully aware from the outset that no contract-between-the-parties exists as can be evidenced by their failure to produce said valid contract upon request, and through process of due diligence carried out by PRA Group (UK) Limited as part of their required duty of care prior to making any contact with myself.

As a result of these actions I have suffered damages.

This charge forms a breach of The Defamation Act 2013.

Negligence

PRA Group (UK) Limited failed routinely to respond to sincere and forthright questions about this matter and have stated on several occasions that they *"will not, and have no obligation to answer said questions"*. This standing demonstrates *secrecy, concealment,* and *failure to disclose* and is not permitted under FCA rules.

PRA Group (UK) Limited abandoned its *due diligence* (in contravention of legislation) and has committed a *breach of duty* with regard to investigating my claims to the fullest extent, and by failing to perform their obligations in a competent and diligent manner.

As a result of these actions I have suffered damages.

This charge will be submitted under a breach of the Torts Act 1977.

Malicious Communications

Since no contract was ever in place between the parties (Barclaycard and myself) regarding a credit facility, it follows that no legitimate contract could be construed out of that failure, between PRA Group (UK) Limited and myself. Therefore ALL communications received from PRA Group (UK) Limited containing requests for payment, threats of collection activity or any mail or calls of any description are malicious in nature and form a comprehensive breach of the Malicious Communications Act 1988.
As a result of these actions I have suffered damages.

Misrepresentation

PRA Group (UK) Limited employed misrepresentation in attempts to coerce me into accepting that there exists a legitimate and enforceable contract between PRA Group (UK) Limited and myself. No contract evidence was produced despite forthright requests.

PRA Group (UK) Limited maintain(ed) an insistence that such a contract does exist and that they have legal standing to pursue me for repayment of the alleged debt, despite their failures in producing said legal authority.

This action forms a comprehensive breach of the Misrepresentation Act 1967.

As a result of these actions I have suffered damages.

Concealment

Fraud by concealment or fraudulent concealment was employed by PRA Group (UK) Limited from the outset whereby false statements and misrepresentations were used throughout the contact process. This was done either deliberately or innocently. Information and proof of claim that I have an absolute right to access under the principle of full disclosure and an obligation of PRA Group (UK) Limited, was entirely absent from the process throughout.

This comprises a breach of the Fraud Act 2006.

As a result of these actions I have suffered damages.

Commercial Damage

As a product of conducting business with Barclaycard, PRA Group (UK) Limited have inflicted damage to my financial standing. Through process of negligent reporting of misinformation to the credit file agencies by PRA Group (UK) Limited, my commercial standing has been impacted considerably. The well-settled obligation within contract law, that ALL processes be halted, whether automatic or not, in the event of a contract dispute or the discovery of a fault in the agreement, until such time as the situation is resolved, has been fully abandoned by PRA Group (UK) Limited as they proceeded to inflict damage without due cause despite my contact with them and raising of the issue.

This comprises a breach of several legislated areas notably:

- The Unfair Contract Terms Act 1977

- The Data Protection Act 2018

- The Fraud Act 2006

And Tort law (Common Law)

As a result of these actions I have suffered damages.

Defamation

PRA Group (UK) Limited registered information with the credit reference agencies that I am a bad debtor – a bad credit risk and have defaulted on contractual obligations. This position is now known to be factually incorrect and those registries false, misleading, and damaging. In the absence of due diligence PRA Group (UK) Limited abandoned their required duty of care and proceeded to make remarks and statements that were entirely untrue. As creditor in the first instance, my standing is impeccable and will always be so. The impact to my credit file is yet more evidence of malfeasance by PRA Group (UK) Limited.

This comprises a comprehensive breach of the Defamation Act 2013.

As a result of these actions I have suffered damages.

Data Protection Breach

Barclaycard collected, stored, manipulated, and disseminated my personal data from the outset of the alleged credit agreement. Since no legitimate contract exists between the parties it therefore follows that there exists NO authority under which Barclaycard can rely upon for holding, processing, and sharing my personal and private information in their database.

Barclaycard NEVER had any legitimate authority for the use of my private and confidential information, and this fact produces a comprehensive breach of the Data

Protection Act 2018 and is being dealt with as a separate matter.

That PRA Group (UK) Limited obtained my personal data from Barclaycard and stored, manipulated, and disseminated it to third parties forms a comprehensive breach of the Data Protection Act 2018, as authority in the matter for PRA Group (UK) Limited to contact me in pursuance an alleged debt through transference of rights, cannot be magically created out of a position where Barclaycard had none.

This forms a comprehensive breach of the Data Protection Act 2018.

As a result of these actions I have suffered damages.

Racketeering

PRA Group (UK) Limited are engaged in the practice of buying bad debts from Barclaycard, or acting upon instruction from Barclaycard and pursuing alleged debtors - as their core business. The methods used are policy driven and occur daily and hourly. That most (if not ALL) alleged 'debt' with Barclaycard can be dismantled via the multiple failures by Barclaycard to conduct their business under current legislation, PRA Group (UK) Limited is therefore engaged in a situation clearly defined under legislation as Racketeering.

This action will be filed under the Proceeds of Crime Act 2002 and the Bribery Act 2010.

As a result of these actions I have suffered damages.

Harassment

PRA Group (UK) Limited engaged in sustained efforts at communication in the form of physical letters to my private address as well as emails to my private email address, making requests / demands for me to pay monies to service an alleged debt that is claimed by them to be subject to a legitimate contract between the parties. PRA Group (UK) Limited also made telephone calls advising that the account would soon attract further action unless payment was made, with an inference that a wrong had been committed by myself and that I should expect unpleasant action as well as damage to my commercial standing in the near future via negative credit file entries.

Any form of contact from an entity unwilling to respond appropriately to inquiry letters in attempts to clarify the situation, and in the absence of a bona fide contractual relationship as its basis, is harassment - particularly contact of a threatening nature.

This matter will be dealt with under the Malicious Communications Act 1988.

As a result of these actions I have suffered damages.

Summary

PRA Group (UK) Limited under the direction of Steven Edward Daws has committed multiple breaches of UK legislation and continues to do so as a matter of company policy.

This behaviour has caused damage to myself and in the wider picture leads to harm and loss for every client / victim of PRA Group (UK) Limited. These breaches are as evident as they are common and must, by virtue of fairness and commercial good-faith be stopped immediately. Several attempts at correcting this matter have been made and all have failed. This failure speaks volumes about PRA Group (UK) Limited under the direction of Steven Edward Daws, and their unwillingness / inability to investigate properly cited faults and failures in their operation, and has steered the course for this action.

Offer

The charges cited within this Notice are fully supported by significant evidence and will be used against PRA Group (UK) Limited to secure remedy and correction of the record if no agreement to settle can be reached. There are several options available for the resolution of this matter:

1. PRA Group (UK) Limited under the direction of Steven Edward Daws makes an apology settlement in the private to me, to produce a full apology, in addition

to retracting all credit file entries made during the course of this matter.

Remedy has been set at a conservative £2m and will produce full and final settlement of the matter in the private. A Non Disclosure agreement, if required, will be duly signed for purposes of keeping the agreement in the private.

2. PRA Group (UK) Limited under the direction of Steven Edward Daws will be cited in a private suit for several charges that have been predetermined to have the best chance of success to claim remedy and produce correction of my status.

3. PRA Group (UK) Limited under the direction of Steven Edward Daws including all executive level persons will be reported to relevant governing bodies and regulatory agencies which will include copies of all evidence, to produce investigations and a public enquiry into the actions of PRA Group (UK) Limited towards its victims.

4. A class action will be served upon PRA Group (UK) Limited. This will undoubtedly become a very public situation and, succeed or fail, will likely create significant impact to PRA Group (UK) Limited's reputation. For some idea of how this operates, a cursory study of the case between Pacific Gas & Electric VS the People of Hinkley, California, might serve to

illustrate what is possible when many people come together with a common goal.

I expect your full co-operation in resolving this matter at this stage, and look forward to receiving your proposal within 28 (twenty eight) days of the date this Notice is received (confirmation by Royal Mail tracking). Failure to respond within the required timeframe will be met with immediate progression to the next phase with full prejudice.

Please note NO extra time will be granted in this matter.

Sincerely

P Michael Yates

Chapter
Twenty Two
Template

Report to Financial Conduct Authority

Samuel Richard Woods
Director Financial Conduct Authority
12 Endeavour Square
London
England
E20 1JN

P Michael Yates
****
****
****
[Postcode]

41st Janbruary 2023

Subject: Formal Complaint Against Barclaycard
For unethical conduct and multiple breaches of UK
legislation

Dear Samuel Richard Woods,

This document comprises my formal complaint against
Barclaycard and Chief Executive Officer Coimbatore
Sundararajan Venkatakrishnan regarding a series of
events recently discovered whilst attempting to open
forthright discussions with the Chief Executive Officer
Coimbatore Sundararajan Venkatakrishnan regarding
Barclaycard's operational policy around credit and
loans.

The issue arose out of the discovery that Barclaycard, as
a matter of bank policy, is routinely disregarding
fundamental laws and legislation in the interests of
profiteering. This practice daily affects the Bank's
customers causing harm and loss (commercial damage)
via incorrect and misleading credit file registries. In
addition, Barclaycard proceed to engage third parties
after-the-fact and supply them with vague or incorrect
information, who then also engage in the practice of

registering incorrect and misleading credit file entries entirely to the detriment of the bank's customer.

Barclaycard have been notified of the situation and have not only elected to ignore my concerns for reasons known only to their executive level, but have instead actively inflicted commercial damage to myself via false and misleading negative entries onto my credit file.

I have enclosed several letters that were sent to Barclaycard's Coimbatore Sundararajan Venkatakrishnan in my attempts to reach a resolution to this matter and will now briefly illustrate the severity of the issue.

1. Barclaycard is routinely failing to adhere to well-settled rules around contract formation. This means that ALL contracts alleged by Barclaycard as being legitimate, binding, and enforceable, between the bank and its customers, are in fact voided from the outset under commercial law. There are NO valid contracts with Barclaycard customers regarding loans / credit and financing that can be produced and enforced in a court of law, because they simply do not exist.

2. Barclaycard is routinely breaching the entirety of the Data Protection Act 2018 due to said failure in securing a valid contract between the parties. Barclaycard has no authority upon which it can

rely for the collection, storage, manipulation, and dissemination of private data belonging to its loan / credit customers. It thus follows that Barclaycard, is holding, processing, and disseminating client data illegally as well as issuing negative credit entries to credit file agencies entirely outside of DPA regulations.

3. Barclaycard routinely breaches the Misrepresentation Act 1967 for failure to issue correct and truthful statements regarding the nature of loans, credit and contracts / agreements. Concealment is an active policy at Barclaycard and forms a serious breach of the Act.

4. Barclaycard routinely breaches the Fraud Act 2006 via fraudulent misrepresentation, fraud by non-disclosure, and fraud by concealment (detailed in attached correspondence to Barclaycard).

5. Barclaycard routinely breaches the Defamation Act 2013 due to its incorrect reporting of breach of contract and missed payments.

6. Barclaycard routinely breaches the Torts Act 1977 via its inability / unwillingness to engage with customers attempting to correct the record regarding the bank's *negligent* actions and failures in *due diligence* in dealing appropriately with legitimate concerns.

7. Barclaycard routinely breaches the Malicious Communications Act 1988 when contacting (via letter, email or telephone) credit / loans customers and making demands for monies to settle an alleged debt.

8. Barclaycard breaches the Theft Act 1978, The Data Protection Act 2018, The Fraud Act 2006 and the Consumer Rights Act 2015 when securitising customers' promissory notes upon credit / loan applications.

9. Barclaycard routinely breaches the Proceeds of Crime Act 2002 and the Bribery Act 2010 due to their policy around credit creation and the alleged contracting / agreement process which is defined under UK legislation as racketeering.

10. Barclaycard routinely breaches the Fraud Act 2006, the Insurance Act 2015, the Proceeds of Crime Act 2002, and the Financial Services and Markets Act 2000 by persistent action regarding insurance policies being created for new credit accounts despite no asset or property of Barclaycard being entered into the pseudo contract as consideration.

11. Barclaycard routinely breach the Protection from Harassment Act 1997 when engaging in any form of contact to credit / loan customers in the absence of legitimate contract.

Barclaycard's comprehensive failure to engage with my correspondence has informed my decision to escalate this issue to the Financial Conduct Authority for further investigation.

I believe that the conduct of Barclaycard may comprise a full contravention of the FCA's regulations and is causing harm to consumers and the integrity of the financial system.

I am hereby notifying you as advised to Barclaycard via Coimbatore Sundararajan Venkatakrishnan and formally request the FCA to investigate this matter thoroughly and take appropriate action to ensure that Barclaycard and its executive officers are penalised until they adhere to the required FCA standards and rectify the issues raised.

Please find enclosed all relevant documentation supporting my claim. I am willing to provide any further information or assistance required during your investigation.

Thank you for your prompt attention to this matter. I look forward to your response and a resolution to this issue.

Sincerely,

P Michael Yates

Chapter Twenty Three

Template

Report to Prudential Regulation Authority

Andrew John Bailey
Governor Bank of England
20 Moorgate
London
England
EC2R 6DA

P Michael Yates
****
****
****
[Postcode]

41st Janbruary 2023

Subject: Formal Complaint Against Barclaycard
For unethical conduct and multiple breaches of UK
legislation

Dear Andrew John Bailey,

This document comprises my formal complaint against
Barclaycard and Chief Executive Officer Coimbatore
Sundararajan Venkatakrishnan under the oversight of
the PRA. It is regarding a series of events recently
discovered whilst attempting to open forthright
discussions with the Chief Executive Officer
Coimbatore Sundararajan Venkatakrishnan regarding
their operational policy around credit and loans.

The issue arose out of the discovery that Barclaycard, as
a matter of bank policy, is routinely disregarding
fundamental laws and legislation in the interests of
profiteering. This practice daily affects the Bank's
customers causing harm and loss (commercial damage)
via incorrect and misleading credit file registries. In
addition, Barclaycard proceed to engage third parties
after-the-fact and supply them with vague or incorrect
information, who then also engage in the practice of

321

registering incorrect and misleading credit file entries entirely at the detriment to the original bank customer.

Barclaycard via Coimbatore Sundararajan have been notified of the situation and have not only elected to ignore my concerns (for reasons known only to their executive level), but have instead actively inflicted commercial damage to myself via false and misleading negative entries onto my credit file.

I have enclosed several letters that were sent to Barclaycard's Coimbatore Sundararajan in my attempts to reach a resolution to this matter and will now briefly illustrate the severity of the issue.

1. Barclaycard is routinely failing to adhere to well-settled rules around contract formation. This means that ALL contracts alleged by Barclaycard as being legitimate, binding, and enforceable, between the bank and its customers are in fact voided from the outset under commercial law. There are NO valid contracts with Barclaycard customers regarding loans / credit and financing that can be produced and enforced in a court of law, because they simply do not exist.

2. Barclaycard is routinely breaching the entirety of the Data Protection Act 2018 – due to said failure in securing a valid contract between the parties. Barclaycard has no authority upon which it can rely for the collection, storage, manipulation, and dissemination of private data belonging to its loan / credit customers. It thus follows that Barclaycard, is issuing negative credit entries to credit file agencies entirely outside of DPA regulations.

3. Barclaycard routinely breaches the Misrepresentation Act 1967 for failure to issue correct and truthful statements regarding the nature of loans, credit and contracts / agreements. Concealment is an active policy at Barclaycard and forms a serious breach of the Act.

4. Barclaycard routinely breaches the Fraud Act 2006 via fraudulent misrepresentation, fraud by non-disclosure, and fraud by concealment (detailed in attached correspondence to Barclaycard).

5. Barclaycard routinely breaches the Defamation Act 2013 due to its incorrect reporting of breach of contract and missed payments.

6. Barclaycard routinely breaches the Torts Act 1977 via its inability / unwillingness to engage with customers attempting to correct the record regarding the bank's *negligence* actions and failures in *due diligence* in dealing appropriately with legitimate concerns.

7. Barclaycard routinely breaches the Malicious Communications Act 1988 when contacting (via letter, email or telephone) credit / loan customers and making demands for monies to settle a non-verified debt.

8. Barclaycard breaches the Theft Act 1978, The Data Protection Act 2018, The Fraud Act 2006 and the Consumer Rights Act 2015 when securitising customers' promissory notes upon credit / loan applications.

9. Barclaycard routinely breaches the Proceeds of Crime Act 2002 and the Bribery Act 2010 due to their policy around credit creation and the alleged contracting / agreement process which is defined under UK legislation as racketeering.

10. Barclaycard routinely breaches the Fraud Act 2006, the Insurance Act 2015, the Proceeds of Crime Act 2002, and the Financial Services and Markets Act 2000 by persistent action regarding insurance policies being created for new credit accounts, despite no asset or property of Barclaycard being entered into the pseudo contract as consideration.

11. Barclaycard routinely breach the Protection from Harassment Act 1997 when engaging in any form of contact to credit / loan customers in the absence of legitimate contract.

Barclaycard's comprehensive failure to engage with my correspondence has informed my decision to escalate this issue to the Financial Conduct Authority for further investigation.

I believe that the conduct of Barclaycard may comprise a full contravention of the PRA's regulations and is causing harm to consumers and the integrity of the financial system.

I am hereby notifying you as advised to Barclaycard via Coimbatore Sundararajan Venkatakrishnan, and formally request the PRA to investigate this matter thoroughly and take appropriate action to ensure that Barclaycard adheres to the required standards and rectifies the issues raised.

Please find enclosed all relevant documentation supporting my claim. I am willing to provide any further information or assistance required during your investigation.

Thank you for your prompt attention to this matter. I look forward to your response and a resolution to this issue.

Sincerely,

P Michael Yates

Chapter
Twenty Four

Template

Report to ICO

John Edwards
Information Commissioner's Office
Wycliffe House
Water Lane
Wilmslow
Cheshire
SK9 5AF

P Michael Yates
****
****
****
[Postcode]

1st Julober 2023

Subject: Formal Notification Against Barclaycard
For Breach of the Data Protection Act 2018

Dear John Edwards,

This document comprises my formal complaint against
Barclaycard and Chief Executive Officer Coimbatore
Sundararajan.

It is regarding a series of events recently discovered
whilst attempting to open forthright discussions with
the Chief Executive Officer Coimbatore Sundararajan
regarding their operational policy around credit and
loans.

The issue arose out of the discovery that Barclaycard, as
a matter of bank policy, is routinely disregarding
fundamental laws and legislation in the interests of
profiteering. This practice daily affects the Bank's
customers and causes harm and loss (commercial
damage) via incorrect and misleading credit file
registries. In addition, Barclaycard engage third parties
after-the-fact and supply them with vague or incorrect

information, who then also engage in the practice of registering incorrect and misleading credit file entries entirely at the detriment to the original bank customer.

Barclaycard via Coimbatore Sundararajan Venkatakrishnan have been notified of the situation and have not only elected to ignore my concerns (for reasons known only to their executive level), but have instead actively inflicted commercial damage to myself via false and misleading negative entries onto my credit file.

I have enclosed several letters that were sent to Barclaycard's Coimbatore Sundararajan Venkatakrishnan in my attempts to reach a resolution to this matter and will now briefly illustrate the severity of the issue.

Barclaycard is routinely failing to adhere to well-settled rules around contract formation. This means that ALL contracts alleged by Barclaycard as being legitimate, binding, and enforceable, between the bank and its customers, are in fact voided from the outset under commercial law. There are NO valid contracts with Barclaycard customers regarding loans / credit and financing that can be produced and enforced in a court of law, because they simply do not exist.

Barclaycard is routinely breaching the entirety of the Data Protection Act 2018 – due to said failure in securing a valid contract between the parties. Barclaycard has no authority upon which it can rely for the collection, storage, manipulation, and dissemination of private data belonging to its loan / credit customers. It thus follows that Barclaycard, is issuing negative credit entries to credit file agencies entirely outside of DPA regulations.

Barclaycard routinely breaches the Misrepresentation Act 1967 for failure to issue correct and truthful statements regarding the nature of loans, credit and contracts / agreements. Concealment is an active policy at Barclaycard and forms a serious breach of the Act.

Barclaycard routinely breaches the Fraud Act 2006 via fraudulent misrepresentation, fraud by non-disclosure, and fraud by concealment (detailed in attached correspondence to Barclaycard).

Barclaycard routinely breaches the Defamation Act 2013 due to its incorrect reporting of breach of contract and missed payments.

Barclaycard routinely breaches the Torts Act 1977 via its inability / unwillingness to engage with customers attempting to correct the record regarding the bank's negligent actions and failures in due diligence in dealing appropriately with legitimate concerns.

Barclaycard routinely breaches the Malicious Communications Act 1988 when contacting (via letter, email or telephone) credit / loan customers and making demands for monies to settle a non-verified debt.

Barclaycard breaches the Theft Act 1978, The Data Protection Act 2018, The Fraud Act 2006 and the Consumer Rights Act 2015 when securitising customers' promissory notes upon credit / loan applications.

Barclaycard routinely breaches the Proceeds of Crime Act 2002 and the Bribery Act 2010 due to their policy around credit creation and the alleged contracting / agreement process which is defined under UK legislation as racketeering.

Barclaycard routinely breaches the Fraud Act 2006, the Insurance Act 2015, the Proceeds of Crime Act 2002, and the Financial Services and Markets Act 2000 by persistent action regarding insurance policies being created for new credit accounts, despite no asset or property of Barclaycard being entered into the pseudo contract as consideration.

Barclaycard routinely breach the Protection from Harassment Act 1997 when engaging in any form of contact to credit / loan customers in the absence of legitimate contract.

Barclaycard's comprehensive failure to engage with my correspondence has informed my decision to escalate this issue to the Financial Conduct Authority for further investigation as well as report their breaches to the ICO. I believe that the conduct of Barclaycard may comprise a full contravention of the Data Protection Act 2018 and is causing harm to consumers and the integrity of the financial system.

I am hereby notifying you as advised to Barclaycard via Coimbatore Sundararajan Venkatakrishnan, and formally request the ICO to investigate this matter thoroughly and take appropriate action to ensure that Barclaycard adheres to the required standards and rectifies the issues raised.

Please find enclosed all relevant documentation supporting my claim. I am willing to provide any further information or assistance required during your investigation.

Thank you for your prompt attention to this matter. I look forward to your response and a resolution to this issue.

Sincerely,
P Michael Yates

Chapter Twenty Five

Template

Lawyer Rebuttal

Selina Burdell
Kearns Solicitors
Brecon House
3 Caerphilly Business Park
Caerphilly
CF83 3GQ

P Michael Yates
****
****
****
****
****

10th Jangust 2022

Your Reference: ##############

Originator Barclaycard
Account Number; **************
Balance £7,668.87

Dear Selina Burdell,

I am in receipt of your letter dated 21 September 2022, entitled 'Letter of Claim' thank you.

I have noted that you are making demands of me.

I require clarification on this matter.

I hereby inform you that the matter you are contacting me about is currently subject to legal proceedings both with your client and the originator of the alleged agreement for comprehensive breaches of United Kingdom legislation in addition to failure to comply with well-settled rules around contract formation.

I have included selections of correspondence where it does not compromise the success of my legal action with the above parties for your consideration, and advise that by aligning yourself with your client and making demands upon me whilst citing my alleged failures under some performance contract or agreement that I have allegedly made with either your client or the originator of this matter, you are exposing yourself to potential prosecution for breach of several areas of UK legislation.

You have also issued a threat should I fail to comply with your demands.

I now require you to validate your standing in this matter that there exists a claim against me based in contractual failure and that your interest in this matter arises out of your completion of due diligence and duty of care, as is legally required of you prior to undertaking this action.

I also require you to produce all of the necessary original documentation as is necessary under law to produce merit in the matter and provide basis for your claim upon me. I am happy to meet with you at a mutually convenient location for my perusal of said ORIGINAL and unmarked documents that will be used to resolve this matter.

Can you verify that LC Asset 2 S.a.r.l. is the holder-in-due-course of the original and unmarked Security Instrument that I would be Redeeming upon settlement of this alleged debt? If the answer is no, then please advise how redemption is possible?

Do you have first-hand knowledge in this matter?

Can you provide me with the name of the person at your office that conducted due diligence prior to the mailing of your letter to me?

I state for the record that there is no dispute. I simply require (as should you) that my suspicions be allayed and that the 'creditor' and subsequent 3rd party interloper after-the-fact, acted appropriately under current legislation and established contracting laws at the onset of this matter.

Please also note that should you fail to validate your claim your letter will be taken as malicious communications along with those from LC Asset 2 S.a.r.l., for which legislation clearly states the following:

Malicious Communications Act 1988:

1 Offence of sending letters etc. with intent to cause distress or anxiety.

>   (1) Any person who sends to another person —

>   (a) a [letter, electronic communication or article of any description] which conveys —

>>   (i) a message which is indecent or grossly offensive;

>>   (ii)   a threat; or

(iii)   information which is false and known or believed to be false by the sender; or

(b) any [article or electronic communication] which is, in whole or part, of an indecent or grossly offensive nature,

is guilty of an offence if his purpose, or one of his purposes, in sending it is that it should, so far as falling within paragraph (a) or (b) above, cause distress or anxiety to the recipient or to any other person to whom he intends that it or its contents or nature should be communicated.

(2) A person is not guilty of an offence by virtue of subsection (1)(a)(ii) above if he shows —

(a) that the threat was used to reinforce a demand [made by him on reasonable grounds]; and

(b) that he believed [and had reasonable grounds for believing,] that the use of the threat was a proper means of reinforcing the demand.

(2A) In this section " electronic communication " includes —

(a) any oral or other communication by means of [an electronic communications network] (c. 12)); and

(d) any communication (however sent) that is in electronic form.]

(3) In this section references to sending include references to delivering [or transmitting] and to causing to be sent [delivered or transmitted] and "sender" shall be construed accordingly.

(4) A person guilty of an offence under this section is liable –

(a) on conviction on indictment to imprisonment for a term not exceeding two years or a fine (or both);

(b) on summary conviction to imprisonment for a term not exceeding 12 months or a fine (or both).

(5) In relation to an offence committed before [paragraph 24(2) of Schedule 22 to the Sentencing Act 2020] comes into force, the reference in subsection (4)(b) to 12 months is to be read as a reference to six months.

(6) In relation to an offence committed before section 85 of the Legal Aid Sentencing and Punishment of Offenders Act 2012 comes into force, the reference in subsection (4)(b) to a fine is to be read as a reference to a fine not exceeding the statutory maximum.]

In the event of your failure to validate your claim and/or by progressing the matter to a (non) court (Northampton Civil National Business Centre etc.) for fictional adjudication, I will assume that your intentions are to employ fraud to gain a pseudo judgment for your client. At this point you and your CEO will be added to the case and face charges for fraud, misrepresentation, extortion, deception, harassment, breach of the data protection act, malicious communications, racketeering, concealment, defamation, and embezzlement.

Please respond to this letter under the Regulatory Framework and Statutory Duty to avoid complications and/or further misrepresentation.

Should you fail to provide basis for your claim against me then I will assume that you are in collusion with LC Asset 2 S.a.r.l., or at the very least, ignorant of the laws and legislation governing contracting and banking, at which point I will take appropriate action to remedy the matter.

Also please note that further communications from you that fail to demonstrate any legal authority to do so will incur charges for my opening, reading, and responding at £150.00 per letter.

Many thanks for your co-operation

Sincerely
P Michael Yates

346

Chapter
Twenty Six

Case Law

There isn't a great deal of case law available involving banks and DCA's being sued for the charges cited in this book and this could be for several reasons including private settlement by the defendant, failures to follow due process by the claimant, the failure by the claimant to be granted merit by the court, and possibly that the consciousness level required to understand the game and embark on this journey is still fresh and requires time to gain traction.

There are however, many cases where banks have been subject to legal action for wrongdoings and the results are available for perusal online. This shows that at some level there are precedents for legal action to be brought against them, but I suspect most attempts have either failed to gain merit or the banks have settled in the private and secured Non Disclosure Agreements with the claimant as part of the settlement.

On that basis, we have at least something to go on that offers hope of reining in our adversary and achieving some form of justice, as however sparse the case law is, at least *something* can be shown.

Not least in this endeavour we have a body of legislation to draw upon that should, if fit for purpose, be suitable to produce what it was conceived to do and restore us to the position we were at prior to our involvement with the banking system.

Should that fail, we will quickly enter brand new territory that will prove (my) suspicions that the line dividing unjust banking practice and our accessing justice, is being upheld by a system standing in direct opposition to our best interests. The illumination of that nugget would likely foster enormous civil unrest and could even tip the scales of societal balance.

In the end, what we all do from here will set the bar for others to follow. To improve upon, refine, and present wider vistas for setting the record straight.

Here are a few citations of case law that show either; that the system is allowing a few cases through to prop-up the illusion of functionality or, that the system works, is available, and stands in opposition to unscrupulous entities that would act outside of it.

1. **Wells Fargo Unauthorized Accounts Scandal**:

In 2016, Wells Fargo faced legal action and regulatory penalties for creating millions of unauthorized customer accounts to meet sales targets. This led to a lawsuit and settlement of around $3 billion.

2. **Goldman Sachs Abacus Mortgage Securities Fraud Case**:

In 2010, the Securities and Exchange Commission (SEC) charged Goldman Sachs with fraud related to the sale of a mortgage investment product called Abacus. This resulted in a settlement of $550 million.

3. **Bank of America Mortgage-Backed Securities Settlement**:

Bank of America faced multiple lawsuits related to the sale of mortgage-backed securities. In 2014, it agreed to a settlement of $16.65 billion to resolve claims of misleading investors about the quality of mortgage-backed securities.

4. **HSBC Money Laundering Case:**

In 2012, HSBC faced allegations of money laundering, including laundering funds for Mexican drug cartels. The bank agreed to a $1.9 billion settlement with authorities.

5. **Barclays Bank PLC v. O'Brien [1994] 1 AC 180:**

This case involved a situation where a wife acted as a guarantor for her husband's debts to Barclays Bank for the purchase of matrimonial property. The wife claimed she had been induced into the transaction due to the bank's misrepresentation of material facts. The House of Lords clarified the principles regarding undue influence, constructive trusts, and the bank's duty to provide accurate information.

6. **Standard Chartered Bank v. Pakistan National Shipping Corporation (No. 2) [2002] EWCA Civ 1643:**

This case dealt with misrepresentation and fraudulent behaviour by the bank. The Court of Appeal discussed the bank's misrepresentation leading to a contract and the consequences of fraudulent behaviour in the banking context.

7. **Green v. Royal Bank of Scotland [2013] EWHC 3671 (QB):**

This case involved a claim against the Royal Bank of Scotland (RBS) for alleged misrepresentation in the sale of an interest rate hedging product. The court found that the bank had made misrepresentations and awarded damages to the claimant.

8. **Graiseley Properties Ltd v. Barclays Bank plc [2013] EWCA Civ 1372:**

In this case, Graiseley Properties sued Barclays Bank for alleged misrepresentation in relation to an interest rate swap agreement. The Court of Appeal found that the bank had made negligent misstatements, ruling in favor of Graiseley Properties and awarding damages.

9. **Plevin v. Paragon Personal Finance Ltd [2014] UKSC 61:**

Although not a case against a bank specifically, this landmark Supreme Court case dealt with misrepresentation and non-disclosure of commissions in payment protection insurance (PPI) sold by banks and financial institutions. The Court ruled in favour of the claimant, Mrs. Plevin, on the grounds of non-disclosure of commission, setting a precedent for many PPI claims.

10. Munir and another v. Bank of Scotland plc [2012] EWHC 2997 (Ch):

This case involved a claim against Bank of Scotland PLC for fraudulent misrepresentation. The High Court found in favour of the claimants, ruling that the bank had engaged in fraudulent misrepresentation and awarded damages.

Final Thoughts

As stated at the beginning of this book, this work is largely theoretical BUT with the added bonus that nothing contained here is conjecture or imagination. Everything is taken directly from established legal foundations and treatise' on common and commercial law. It is the considered *application* of what is stated under legislation through the methods advised IN the legislation.

If the applicable pre-action protocols and required process are followed to the letter – according to *their* rules, then one should reasonably expect a favourable outcome in line with what has been 'decreed'.

If our remedy is not forthcoming and subsequently the relevant governing bodies fail to take the action they're required to take, then we'll be in uncharted territory. If that situation is allowed to develop then the system we live under faces being exposed as a sham and will be shown positively to have failed in adhering to its own rules.

If that situation ever arises it'll be anyone's guess as to what will happen next. At the very least it will reveal what I've long suspected - that Parliament is ineffective and exists purely to present a thin veneer of justice and democratic governance to convince us all that we live in a fair and caring place (despite what most can see with their own eyes), whilst those that are part of the gang continue to milk the energy of ordinary people to maintain themselves in opulence.

The entirety of government will shudder when average men & women come into the realisation that a pre-selected group of people are living quite extraordinary lives on the backs of every one of us. The situation is nothing new and the political class are well-accustomed to having this levelled at them from the side-lines, and every other Hollywood movie features a villain at the top sucking the energy out of everyone below.

It seems that this scenario is the norm for human life as almost every culture operates a similar theme across the world. And it *has* been going on for a long time, but I know, as well as most readers of this book – changes are afoot. The establishment knows it too and are frantically trying to keep a lid on the soon-to-boil-pot of absolute frustration and desperate desire for change. The change may come sooner than most think, but it won't be without pain and will certainly carry a price. In the meantime, we have to correct the situation as best we can by bringing all situations back to law – the law that was implemented for our guidance.

So private settlement is obviously the preferred option as a resolution to our situation, as it will enable the banking system to continue (albeit as a slightly less profitable version) whilst producing remedy for all those that can be bothered to aim for justice and a fairer situation.

In the event that the banks fail to see the upside of settling in the private, and by their own choice elect to do it the hard way, let's hope that the system gets its *Act* together and enforces that which it claims to uphold before the inevitable storm arrives.

The days are very definitely numbered for the continuation of the banking system as it currently exists, and that's without factoring in the work Debt Ninjas are doing. I would hope that there are some executive-level personnel that still care enough about their fellow men & women to drive changes that are more aligned to a fairer and less secretive financial system. It really boils down to them acting for the greater good despite a short-term painful episode.

In the meantime there's a job to be done and I for one am playing my part in it. By the looks of things, very many others are stepping up too, and that can only be a good thing as it's essentially a numbers game. The more Debt Ninjas taking the banks to task, the more the story spreads, and the more it informs the banks that they are on a very short leash regarding how far they can push it now.

Whilst I'm on the subject of taking the banks to task, I'll address a common myth surrounding what we do at Debt Ninjas. "You'll end up in big trouble for doing all this – the banks WILL NOT tolerate it."

Really?

Well, here's the deal. A bank with a new customer for a credit card takes the security instrument and makes profit from it. The customer then either pays the account monthly in ignorance of what happened – usually for life, OR fails to make the payment through hardship or because they came across some information and realised that the whole deal is a sham.

When the bank retains an old customer they only get one agreement to securitise, but when another customer (after following the process) continually makes new agreements with the bank, there's a potentially limitless amount of securities that can be created, and the bank makes even more money. Yes they'll have to share that money with the customer for providing original issue securities, but that's an infinitely better way of discharging the alleged national debt and creating new wealth than the current method. Prove me wrong!

I guess that this will be the final book on this subject as the tools are all here for the use of, but I never say never, so let's see what comes out of this. There will be updates I'm sure, but the meat of it is here. All of the essential reading and links to the heavyweight contract law books can be found on the Facebook private group and the forum on the website - and by being in those groups you'll get access to some of the sharpest minds I've ever encountered regarding this subject.

I wish you well on your journey and that this book awakens the hunger for justice and launches a start on fixing the problems we all endure on a daily basis.

Thanks for reading and cheers to ALL Debt Ninjas!

Help, support, and community

https://debt-ninjas.com/

info@debt-ninjas.com

debtninjas@gmail.com

https://www.facebook.com/groups/641253403157261

Made in United States
Troutdale, OR
10/01/2024

23279880R00199